HOLT SCIENCE & TECHNOLOGY

Life Science

REINFORCEMENT & VOCABULARY REVIEW WORKSHEETS

This book was printed with soy-based ink on acid-free recycled content paper, containing 10% POSTCONSUMER WASTE.

HOLT, RINEHART AND WINSTON

A Harcourt Classroom Education Company

Austin • New York • Orlando • Atlanta • San Francisco • Boston • Dallas • Toronto • London

W9-AWT-584

To the Teacher

These worksheets are designed to help you reinforce the vocabulary and concepts students need to build a solid foundation in the sciences. Key concepts are reviewed in the Reinforcement Worksheets. Key terms are stressed in the Vocabulary Review Worksheets. This booklet contains one Vocabulary Review Worksheet and at least one Reinforcement Worksheet for each chapter in the *Holt Science and Technology* Pupil's Edition.

■ REINFORCEMENT WORKSHEETS

By approaching a topic that is discussed in the Pupil's Edition from a different angle, such as with visual aids or within the framework of a new scenario, these worksheets help move students from frustration to understanding. You can use Reinforcement Worksheets to do the following:

• target the students in the class who are struggling to understand a concept;
• gauge how well the class is understanding a topic before you formally assess the topic or before you move on to a new, progressive topic;
• provide a refresher of a topic discussed in the last class period;
• conclude a lesson by having students revisit and reinforce an essential topic;
• instill confidence as students complete these enjoyable and doable worksheets;
• provide opportunities for group work and cooperative learning.

■ VOCABULARY REVIEW WORKSHEETS

With puzzles, crosswords, word searches, and other nonintimidating challenges, the Vocabulary Review Worksheets can help your students do the following:

• remember important vocabulary terms from each chapter;
• review and study vocabulary definitions;
• think critically about the way in which the words are used in talking about science;
• warm up for a new lesson by starting out with a puzzle;
• participate in cooperative learning activities by solving puzzles with a partner or group.

ANSWER KEY

For your convenience, an answer key is provided in the back of this booklet. The key includes reduced versions of all applicable worksheets with answers included.

Copyright © by Holt, Rinehart and Winston

All rights reserved. No part of this publication may be reproduced or transmitted in any form or by any means, electronic or mechanical, including photocopy, recording, or any information storage and retrieval system, without permission in writing from the publisher.

Teachers using HOLT SCIENCE AND TECHNOLOGY may photocopy student activity sheets in complete pages in sufficient quantities for classroom use only and not for resale.

Art and Photo Credits
All work, unless otherwise noted, contributed by Holt, Rinehart and Winston.
Abbreviated as follows: (t) top; (b) bottom; (l) left; (r) right; (c) center; (bkgd) background.
Front Cover (owl), Kim Taylor/Bruce Coleman, Inc.; (forest), Carr Clifton; (jaguar), ©Gerry Ellis/GerryEllis.com; Page 35 (tr), David Kelly; 37 (b), David Kelly; 38 (b), David Kelly; 39 (t), Carlyn Iverson; 40 (tr), Carlyn Iverson; 69 (c), Carlyn Iverson; 70 (c), Carlyn Iverson

Printed in the United States of America

ISBN 0-03-055408-X   1 2 3 4 5 6 7   085   04 03 02 01 00

• CONTENTS •

WORKSHEET	SUGGESTED POINT OF USE	PAGE
CHAPTER 1: THE WORLD OF LIFE SCIENCE		
Reinforcement: The Mystery of the Bubbling Top	Section 2	1
Vocabulary Review: The Puzzling World of Life Science	End of Chapter	3
CHAPTER 2: IT'S ALIVE!! OR, IS IT?		
Reinforcement: Amazing Discovery	Section 2	5
Reinforcement: Building Blocks	Section 3	6
Vocabulary Review: It's Alive!	End of Chapter	7
CHAPTER 3: CELLS: THE BASIC UNITS OF LIFE		
Reinforcement: An Ecosystem	Section 1	9
Reinforcement: Building a Eukaryotic Cell	Section 3	10
Vocabulary Review: A Cell Crossword Puzzle	End of Chapter	11
CHAPTER 4: THE CELL IN ACTION		
Reinforcement: Into and Out of the Cell	Section 1	13
Reinforcement: Activities of the Cell	Section 2	14
Reinforcement: This Is Radio KCEL	Section 3	15
Vocabulary Review: Cell Game Show	End of Chapter	16
CHAPTER 5: HEREDITY		
Reinforcement: Dimples and DNA	Section 1	17
Vocabulary Review: Vocabulary Garden	End of Chapter	19
CHAPTER 6: GENES AND GENE TECHNOLOGY		
Reinforcement: DNA Mutations	Section 2	21
Vocabulary Review: Unraveling Genes	End of Chapter	23
CHAPTER 7: EVOLUTION OF LIVING THINGS		
Reinforcement: Bicentennial Celebration	Section 2	25
Vocabulary Review: Charles Darwin's Legacy	End of Chapter	26
CHAPTER 8: THE HISTORY OF LIFE ON EARTH		
Reinforcement: Earth Timeline	Section 1	27
Reinforcement: Condensed History	Section 2	28
Vocabulary Review: Mary Leakey's Search	End of Chapter	29
CHAPTER 9: CLASSIFICATION		
Reinforcement: Keys to the Kingdom	Section 2	31
Vocabulary Review: Classification Clues	End of Chapter	33

WORKSHEET	SUGGESTED POINT OF USE	PAGE
CHAPTER 10: BACTERIA AND VIRUSES		
Reinforcement: Bacteria Bonanza	Section 1	35
Reinforcement: The Lytic Cycle	Section 3	36
Vocabulary Review: A Puzzle of Tiny Things	End of Chapter	37
CHAPTER 11: PROTISTS AND FUNGI		
Reinforcement: Protists on Parade	Section 1	39
Reinforcement: An Ode to a Fungus	Section 2	40
Vocabulary Review: A Moldy Puzzle	End of Chapter	41
CHAPTER 12: INTRODUCTION TO PLANTS		
Reinforcement: Classifying Plants	Section 3	43
Reinforcement: Drawing Dicots	Section 3	44
Vocabulary Review: Those Puzzling Plants	End of Chapter	45
CHAPTER 13: PLANT PROCESSES		
Reinforcement: Fertilizing Flowers	Section 1	47
Reinforcement: A Leaf's Work Is Never Done	Section 2	48
Reinforcement: How Plants Respond to Change	Section 3	49
Vocabulary Review: Scrambled Plants	End of Chapter	50
CHAPTER 14: ANIMALS AND BEHAVIOR		
Reinforcement: What Makes an Animal an Animal?	Section 1	51
Reinforcement: Animal Interviews	Section 2	52
Vocabulary Review: Puzzling Animal Behavior	End of Chapter	53
CHAPTER 15: INVERTEBRATES		
Reinforcement: Life Without a Backbone	Section 1	55
Reinforcement: Spineless Variety	Section 4	56
Vocabulary Review: Searching for a Backbone	End of Chapter	57
CHAPTER 16: FISHES, AMPHIBIANS, AND REPTILES		
Reinforcement: Coldblooded Critters	Section 4	59
Vocabulary Review: Fishin' for Vertebrates	End of Chapter	61
CHAPTER 17: BIRDS AND MAMMALS		
Reinforcement: Mammals Are Us	Section 2	63
Vocabulary Review: Is It a Bird or a Mammal?	End of Chapter	64

CONTENTS, CONTINUED

WORKSHEET	SUGGESTED POINT OF USE	PAGE
CHAPTER 18: INTERACTIONS OF LIVING THINGS		
Reinforcement: Weaving a Food Web	Section 2	65
Reinforcement: Symbiotic Relationships	Section 3	66
Vocabulary Review: Environmental Enigma	End of Chapter	67
CHAPTER 19: CYCLES IN NATURE		
Reinforcement: What Goes Around . . .	Section 1	69
Vocabulary Review: Cycle Search	End of Chapter	71
CHAPTER 20: THE EARTH'S ECOSYSTEMS		
Reinforcement: Know Your Biomes	Section 1	73
Vocabulary Review: Eco-Puzzle	End of Chapter	75
CHAPTER 21: ENVIRONMENTAL PROBLEMS AND SOLUTIONS		
Reinforcement: It's "R" Planet!	Section 2	77
Vocabulary Review: Solve the Environmental Puzzle	End of Chapter	79
CHAPTER 22: BODY ORGANIZATION AND STRUCTURE		
Reinforcement: The Hipbone's Connected to the . . .	Section 2	81
Reinforcement: Muscle Map	Section 3	82
Vocabulary Review: A Connective Crossword	End of Chapter	83
CHAPTER 23: CIRCULATION AND RESPIRATION		
Reinforcement: Matchmaker, Matchmaker	Section 1	85
Reinforcement: Colors of the Heart	Section 1	86
Vocabulary Review: A Hunt with Heart	End of Chapter	87
CHAPTER 24: THE DIGESTIVE AND URINARY SYSTEMS		
Reinforcement: Annie Apple's Amazing Adventure	Section 2	89
Vocabulary Review: Alien Anagrams	End of Chapter	90
CHAPTER 25: COMMUNICATION AND CONTROL		
Reinforcement: This System Is Just "Two" Nervous!	Section 1	91
Reinforcement: The Eyes Have It	Section 2	93
Reinforcement: Every Gland Lends a Hand	Section 3	94
Vocabulary Review: Your Body's Own Language	End of Chapter	95

WORKSHEET	SUGGESTED POINT OF USE	PAGE
CHAPTER 26: REPRODUCTION AND DEVELOPMENT		
Reinforcement: Reproduction Review	Section 1	97
Reinforcement: The Beginning of a Life	Section 3	98
Vocabulary Review: A Reproduction Crossword	End of Chapter	99
CHAPTER 27: BODY DEFENSES AND DISEASE		
Reinforcement: Immunity Teamwork	Section 2	101
Vocabulary Review: Puzzle-itis Vaccine	End of Chapter	102
CHAPTER 28: STAYING HEALTHY		
Reinforcement: To Eat or Not to Eat . . .	Section 1	103
Vocabulary Review: Hidden Health Message	End of Chapter	105
ANSWER KEY		107

Name _____ Date _____ Class_____

1 REINFORCEMENT WORKSHEET

The Mystery of the Bubbling Top

Complete this worksheet after you finish reading Chapter 1, Section 2.
Use the materials at right to conduct the activity below. Then
answer the questions that follow.

<table>
<tr><td>MATERIALS</td></tr>
</table>

MATERIALS
- small, empty, plastic soda bottle
- cold water
- plastic or plastic-foam disposable plate
- scissors
- hot water
- beaker or other container large enough to hold the soda bottle

1. Fill the empty bottle halfway with cold water.

2. Cut a quarter-sized disk from the plastic plate.

3. Moisten the plastic disk, and place it on top of the bottle's neck.

4. Pour hot water into the beaker until it is about one-quarter full.

5. Carefully place the bottle inside the beaker.

6. What happened to the plastic disk?

_____

_____

_____

You just made observations.

7. Why do you think the plastic disk did that? Brainstorm for as many answers as possible. Then put a star next to the explanation you consider most reasonable.

_____

_____

_____

_____

You just formed a hypothesis.

8. How could you test your hypothesis? Outline an experiment you could conduct.

_____

_____

_____

_____

Copyright © by Holt, Rinehart and Winston. All rights reserved.

REINFORCEMENT & VOCABULARY REVIEW WORKSHEETS **1**

The Mystery of the Bubbling Top, continued

---

9. Conduct your experiment. What happened?

_____

_____

You just tested your hypothesis.

10. How do you explain the results of your experiment?

_____

_____

_____

_____

You just analyzed the results of your experiment.

11. Do the results of your experiment match your hypothesis? Explain.

_____

_____

_____

_____

12. Do you need to conduct more experiments to find out if your hypothesis is correct? Why or why not?

_____

_____

_____

_____

_____

You just drew conclusions.

Congratulations!
You have just finished the first steps of the scientific method!
Share your results with your classmates.

Copyright © by Holt, Rinehart and Winston. All rights reserved.

CHAPTER

1 VOCABULARY REVIEW WORKSHEET

The Puzzling World of Life Science

Try this puzzle after you finish reading Chapter 1.
Using each of these clues, fill in the blanks provided on the next page with the letters of the word or phrase described below.

1. the use of knowledge, tools, and materials to solve problems and accomplish tasks

2. a unifying explanation for a broad range of hypotheses and observations that have been supported by testing

3. the measure of an object's surface

4. liquid that freezes at 0°C and boils at 100°C

5. the amount of space that something occupies

6. used for almost a century to see internal body structures

7. A _____ _____ tests one factor at a time.

8. made before scientists can test a hypothesis, stated as "if . . . , then . . ."

9. A _____ _____ microscope has a tube with lenses, a stage, and a light source.

10. the study of living things

11. Scientists draw _____ after analyzing data from experiments.

12. the one factor that differs in a controlled experiment

13. set of steps scientists use to answer a question or solve a problem

14. measured in Kelvins or degrees Celsius

15. the amount of matter that makes up an object

16. anything in an experiment that can influence the outcome of the experiment

17. uses short bursts of a magnetic field to produce images (abbreviation)

18. possible answer to a question

19. uses electrons to produce magnified images

20. Scientists _____ their results to other scientists after they complete their investigations.

21. common unit of length in SI

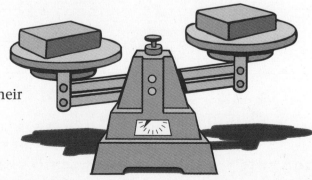

Copyright © by Holt, Rinehart and Winston. All rights reserved.

The Puzzling World of Life Science, continued

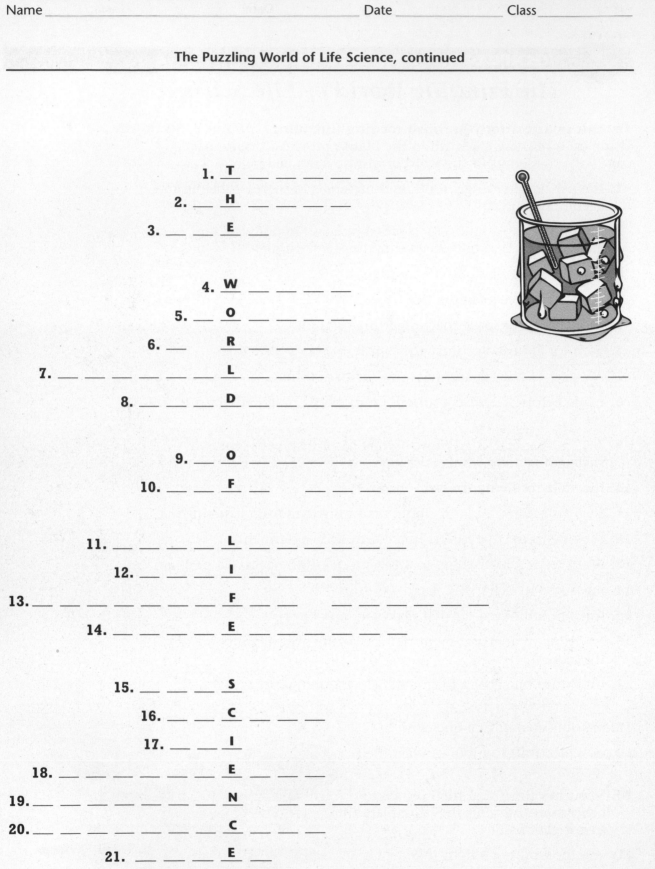

1. **T** __ __ __ __ __ __ __ __ __ __

2. __ **H** __ __ __ __ __

3. __ __ **E** __

4. **W** __ __ __ __

5. __ **O** __ __ __ __

6. __ **R** __ __ __

7. __ __ __ __ __ **L** __ __ __   __ __ __ __ __ __ __ __ __

8. __ __ **D** __ __ __ __ __

9. __ **O** __ __ __ __ __   __ __ __ __

10. __ __ **F** __   __ __ __ __ __ __

11. __ __ __ **L** __ __ __ __ __

12. __ __ __ **I** __ __ __ __

13. __ __ __ __ __ **F** __ __   __ __ __ __ __ __

14. __ __ __ **E** __ __ __ __ __

15. __ __ __ **S**

16. __ __ **C** __

17. __ __ **I**

18. __ __ __ __ **E** __ __ __

19. __ __ __ __ **N** __   __ __ __ __ __ __ __ __

20. __ __ __ **C** __ __ __

21. __ __ __ **E** __

Copyright © by Holt, Rinehart and Winston. All rights reserved.

Name _____ Date _____ Class _____

Amazing Discovery

Complete this worksheet after you finish reading Chapter 2, Section 2.

Imagine that you are a biologist on a mission to Mars. You have just discovered what you think is a simple single-celled Martian organism. For now, you are calling it Alpha. Before you can claim that you have discovered life on Mars, however, you need to show that Alpha is alive.

1. What are the six characteristics you will look for to see if Alpha is alive?

a. _____

b. _____

c. _____

d. _____

e. _____

f. _____

2. Outline a test or experiment to verify one of the characteristics you listed above.

_____

_____

_____

_____

_____

_____

_____

3. If you can show that Alpha is alive, you will take it back to Earth for further study. What will you need to provide Alpha with to keep it alive?

_____

_____

_____

Copyright © by Holt, Rinehart and Winston. All rights reserved.

CHAPTER

2 **REINFORCEMENT WORKSHEET**

Building Blocks

Complete this worksheet after you finish reading Chapter 2, Section 3.

Each of the boxes below represents one of the five compounds that are found in all cells. The phrases at the bottom of the page describe these compounds. Match each of the descriptions to the appropriate compound. Then write the corresponding letter in the appropriate box. Some descriptions may be used more than once.

Compounds in Cells

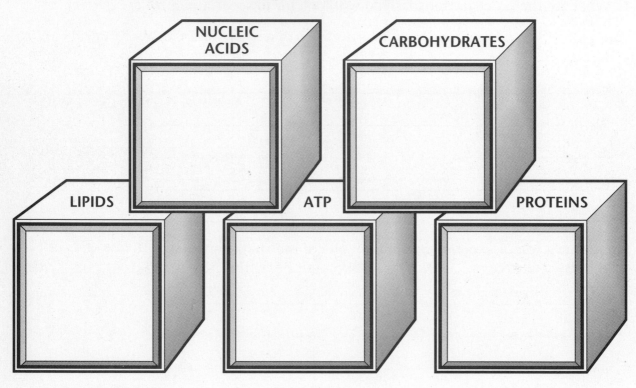

Clues

A. fat in animals

B. made of sugars

C. oil in plants

D. one type forms much of the cell membrane

E. enzymes

F. major fuel used for the cell's activities

G. "blueprints" of life

H. subunits are amino acids

I. hemoglobin

J. cannot mix with water

K. DNA

L. tells the cell how to make proteins

M. can be simple or complex

N. subunits called nucleotides

O. make up spider webs and hair

P. starch in plants

Q. source of stored energy

R. adenosine triphosphate

S. energy in lipids and carbohydrates is transferred to this molecule

Copyright © by Holt, Rinehart and Winston. All rights reserved.

Name _____ Date _____ Class _____

It's Alive!

Complete this puzzle after you finish Chapter 2.

In the space provided, write the term described by the clue. Then find these words in the puzzle. Terms can be hidden in the puzzle vertically, horizontally, diagonally, or backward.

1. _____ change in an organism's environment that affects the activity of an organism

2. _____ group of compounds made of sugars

3. _____ maintenance of a stable internal environment

4. _____ complex carbohydrate made by plants

5. _____ transmission of characteristics from one generation to the next

6. _____ chemical activities of an organism necessary for life

7. _____ made up of subunits called nucleotides

8. _____ eats other organisms for food

9. _____ organism that breaks down the nutrients of dead organisms or wastes for food

10. _____ two layers of these form much of the cell membrane

11. _____ proteins that speed up certain chemical reactions

12. _____ molecule that provides instructions for making proteins

13. _____ organism that can produce its own food

14. _____ membrane-covered structure that contains all materials necessary for life

15. _____ reproduction in which a single parent produces offspring that are identical to the parent

16. _____ chemical compound that cannot mix with water and that is used to store energy

17. _____ large molecule made up of amino acids

18. _____ energy in food is transferred to this molecule

19. _____ reproduction in which two parents are necessary to produce offspring that share characteristics of both parents

Copyright © by Holt, Rinehart and Winston. All rights reserved.

It's Alive! continued

D	P	H	O	S	P	H	O	L	I	P	I	D	S
N	S	D	T	E	R	P	U	I	R	C	S	E	I
A	A	S	E	X	U	A	L	O	O	I	T	C	S
R	C	Y	Z	U	P	H	D	S	T	A	I	O	A
C	E	L	L	A	T	U	E	D	R	B	M	M	T
O	N	M	X	L	C	H	C	D	E	D	U	P	S
N	Z	E	H	E	C	E	Y	I	I	P	L	O	O
S	Y	O	R	R	I	H	A	P	L	L	U	S	E
U	M	N	A	R	O	L	I	U	X	C	S	E	M
M	E	T	A	B	O	L	I	S	M	Y	U	R	O
E	S	E	R	L	N	P	R	O	T	E	I	N	H
R	H	A	M	Z	Y	T	I	D	E	R	E	H	E
A	C	E	D	I	C	A	C	I	E	L	C	U	N

Copyright © by Holt, Rinehart and Winston. All rights reserved.

Name _____ Date _____ Class_____

An Ecosystem

Complete this worksheet after you finish reading Chapter 3, Section 1.
Examine the picture below. It shows living and nonliving things
existing in an ecosystem. Fill in the table to describe the organization
of this ecosystem.

Nonliving things	Populations

1. What makes up the community in this ecosystem?

_____

_____

_____

_____

Copyright © by Holt, Rinehart and Winston. All rights reserved.

CHAPTER

3 REINFORCEMENT WORKSHEET

Building a Eukaryotic Cell

Complete this worksheet after you finish reading Chapter 3, Section 3.
Below is a list of the features found in eukaryotic cells. Next to each
feature, write a *P* if it is a feature found only in plant cells and a *B* if
it is a feature that can be found in both plant and animal cells.

1. _____ endoplasmic reticulum   **8.** _____ Golgi complex

2. _____ mitochondria   **9.** _____ cell wall

3. _____ nucleus   **10.** _____ vesicles

4. _____ large vacuole   **11.** _____ DNA

5. _____ cell membrane   **12.** _____ nucleolus

6. _____ cytoplasm   **13.** _____ chloroplasts

7. _____ ribosomes

In the space provided, label the structures of the eukaryotic cell
drawn below. Include all of the structures that you labeled *B*.

A Eukaryotic Cell

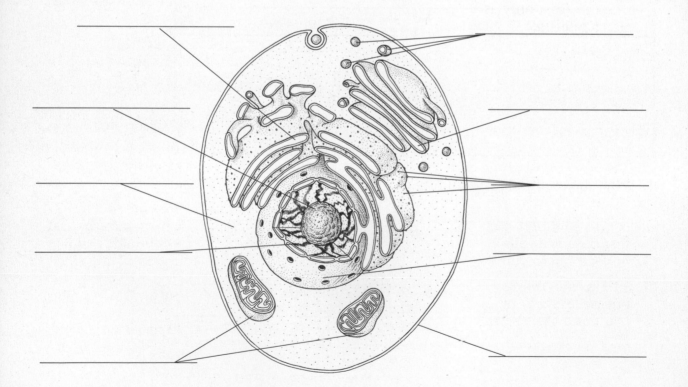

Copyright © by Holt, Rinehart and Winston. All rights reserved.

CHAPTER

3 VOCABULARY REVIEW WORKSHEET

A Cell Crossword Puzzle

Try this puzzle after finishing Chapter 3.
Use the clues below to complete the crossword puzzle on the next page.

ACROSS

1. the fluid inside a cell

6. another name for 12 across

9. the control center of a cell

11. special vesicles containing enzymes

12. cells that do not have a nucleus

14. organelle that modifies, packages, and transports materials out of the cell

18. describes an organism that can exist only as a group of cells

22. A single _____ has all of the items necessary to carry out life's activities.

23. a combination of two or more tissues working together to perform a specific job in the body

25. british scientist who first observed cells under a microscope

26. energy-converting organelle found in plant and algae cells

27. anything that can live on its own

28. groups of organs working together to perform particular jobs in the body

29. one of the structures a cell uses to live, grow, and reproduce

DOWN

1. all of the populations of different species that live and interact in an area

2. The cells of plants and algae have a hard _____ _____ made of cellulose.

3. organelles at which amino acids are hooked together to make proteins

4. the cell's hereditary material

5. a group of similar cells that work together to do a specific job in the body

7. cells that have a central nucleus and a complicated inner structure

8. All eukaryotic cells have membrane-covered compartments called _____ that form when part of the cell membrane surrounds an object and pinches off.

10. a group of the same kind of organisms that live in the same area at the same time

13. the cell's power plants; break down food molecules to make ATP

15. barrier between the inside of a cell and its environment

16. dark spot inside the nucleus that stores the materials that will be used later to make ribosomes

17. three statements that define all living things in terms of cells

19. the cell's delivery system (abbr.)

20. special molecule that provides energy for a cell's activities

21. a community and all of the nonliving things that affect it

24. a large membrane-covered chamber that stores liquids and is found in plant cells

Copyright © by Holt, Rinehart and Winston. All rights reserved.

A Cell Crossword Puzzle, continued

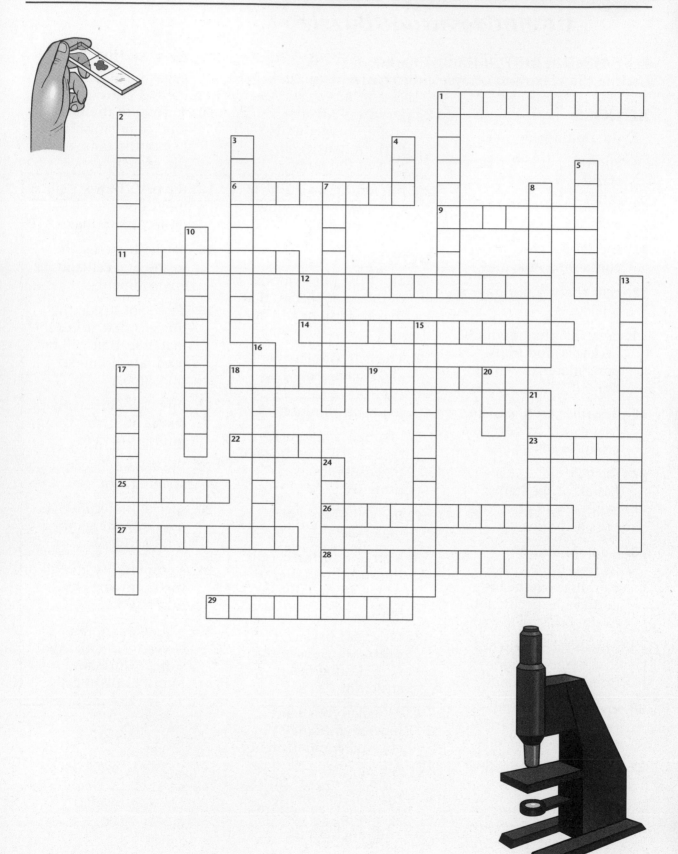

Copyright © by Holt, Rinehart and Winston. All rights reserved.

CHAPTER

4 **REINFORCEMENT WORKSHEET**

Into and Out of the Cell

Complete this worksheet after you have finished reading Chapter 4, Section 1.

Each of the boxes below represents a different method cells use to bring small particles into the cell or to take small particles out of the cell. Add the notes at the bottom of the page to the appropriate box. Be careful—some notes can be used more than once.

Small Particle Transport

Osmosis	Passive Transport	Active Transport

Notes

- particles move through protein doorways
- particles move through cell membrane between phospholipid molecules
- sugar or amino acids

- requires ATP
- particles move from an area of high concentration to an area of low concentration
- does not require ATP

- particles move from an area of low concentration to an area of high concentration
- water

Copyright © by Holt, Rinehart and Winston. All rights reserved.

CHAPTER
4 **REINFORCEMENT WORKSHEET**

Activities of the Cell

Complete this worksheet after you have finished reading Chapter 4, Section 2.

1. Sketch and label a chloroplast and a mitochondrion in the space provided.

2. Chloroplasts use light energy during photosynthesis. To your drawing add a light source and an arrow from the light source to the chloroplast.

3. Chloroplasts give off oxygen and glucose during photosynthesis. Mitochondria use oxygen and glucose during cellular respiration. Add this information to your diagram.

4. During cellular respiration, mitochondria produce ATP. Add this information to your diagram.

5. Besides light energy, what do chloroplasts use to make glucose?

_____

_____

6. Besides ATP, what do mitochondria give off during cellular respiration?

_____

_____

7. Add the information from questions 5 and 6 to your diagram.

Copyright © by Holt, Rinehart and Winston. All rights reserved.

This is Radio KCEL

Complete this worksheet after you have finished reading Chapter 4, Section 3.

Hello, Cell-O-Rama radio fans! Katy Chromosome here. We have a very exciting program in store for you: *Cell Mitosis in Action,* with local sports announcers Sid Toekinesis and Dee Ennay. To make this a Cell-O-Rama challenge, we've spliced the sound clips from each phase of mitosis in the wrong order. Your job is to identify the correct phase for each clip and then put the clips in the correct sequence. Good luck! Dee and Sid?

Sid: Thanks, Katy. Let's roll the tape, Dee.

Dee: Rolling . . .

Segment A: Mitosis Phase _____

Sid: Dee, I think the Chromatid twins are really mad this time. They seem to be storming off in opposite directions. Don't they care about the game?

Dee: This is just incredible, Sid. Wait a minute! Both groups appear to be moving into huddles. Is the game over? Do you think they'll come back?

Segment B: Mitosis Phase _____

Sid: Dee, this is UN-believable. The Chromatid twins are shrinking! Are they getting ready for a fight?

Dee: Sid, I am brand new to this game, and I just don't know what might happen next. Where on *Earth* are those centrioles going?

Sid: Dee, I think things are getting too hot for them. They are hightailing it out of there.

Dee: Oh no. They seem to be throwing a net to trap the Chromatid twins. It looks like the centrioles are herding them to the center of the field.

Segment C: Mitosis Phase _____

Sid: This is truly amazing, Dee. Some sort of barrier seems to be forming around each of the huddles. What is going on?

Dee: Sid, believe it or not, I think the teams are taking a timeout. See how they're all unwinding? They have worked hard today. This has been *quite* a game!

Segment D: Mitosis Phase _____

Sid: Dee, maybe they're getting ready for a kickoff. The twins are lining up along the center of the field. I think they're waiting for a signal.

Dee: Sid, you can just *feel* the tension in the air. Uh oh. I think a fight just broke out. Wait—they're all *wrestling* out there! The twins look like they're trying to get away from each other. Where are the refs when you need them?

Copyright © by Holt, Rinehart and Winston. All rights reserved.

CHAPTER
4 VOCABULARY REVIEW WORKSHEET

Cell Game Show

After you finish Chapter 4, give this puzzle a try!

This game may be played individually or in teams. You are supplied with the answers to questions in four categories. Your challenge is to come up with the correct question for each answer. Each correct "question" has a point value corresponding to the number at the beginning of the row. Keep a running total of your points as you play.

	To Make Two	On the Move	Lazy Days	I Can "C" You
50	These condense into an X-shape before mitosis.	How a cell membrane moves large particles into the cell	The movement of particles from an area of high concentration to an area of low concentration	This process ends when a cell divides and new cells are formed.
100	Human body cells have 23 pairs of these.	The movement of particles through proteins against the normal direction of diffusion	Oxygen can slip between these molecules, which make up much of the cell membrane.	This is the region where chromatids are held together.
200	Bacteria double this way.	This word means "outside the cell."	Diffusion of water across a membrane	The way organisms get energy from food using oxygen
500	The complicated process of chromosome separation; the second stage of the cell cycle	The process by which plants capture light energy and change it into food	The diffusion of particles through special "doorways" in the cell membrane	The cytoplasm splits in two during this process.
1000	During the third stage of the cell cycle, this forms in eukaryotic cells with cell walls.	When there's no oxygen for your cells, they use this to get energy.	Special doorways in the cell membrane are made of these.	Oxygen can pass directly through this cell part.

Total Points: _____

Copyright © by Holt, Rinehart and Winston. All rights reserved.

CHAPTER
5 **REINFORCEMENT WORKSHEET**

Dimples and DNA

Complete this worksheet after you have finished reading Chapter 5, Section 1.

In humans, dimpled cheeks are a dominant trait, with a genotype of **DD** or **Dd.** Nondimpled cheeks are a recessive trait, with a genotype of **dd.**

1. Imagine that Parent A, with the genotype **DD**, has dimpled cheeks. Parent B has the genotype **dd** and does not have dimpled cheeks.

 The Punnett square below diagrams the cross between Parent A and Parent B. Complete the Punnett square. (The first square has been done for you. You may want to refer to How to Make a Punnett square in your text.)

Parent A

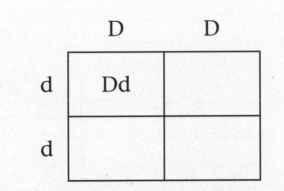

2. A Punnett square shows what genotypes are possible for the offspring of a certain cross. What genotypes are possible for the offspring of Parent A and Parent B?

_____

_____

3. Each of the four squares of a Punnett square represents a 25 per-cent probability that the offspring will have that particular genotype. What is the probability that the offspring of Parent A and Parent B will have dimpled cheeks?

_____

_____

_____

Copyright © by Holt, Rinehart and Winston. All rights reserved.

___

Dimples and DNA, continued

4. Parent X, with the genotype *Dd,* has dimpled cheeks. Parent Y also has the genotype *Dd* and has dimpled cheeks as well. To find out what their offspring might look like, complete the Punnett square below.

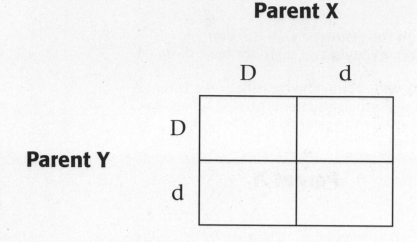

Parent X

Parent Y

5. What is the probability that the offspring of Parent X and Parent Y will have each of the following genotypes?

DD: _____

Dd: _____

dd: _____

6. What is the probability that the offspring of Parent X and Parent Y will have nondimpled cheeks?

_____

_____

7. What is the probability that the offspring of Parent X and Parent Y will have dimpled cheeks? (Remember that there are two genotypes that can produce dimpled cheeks.)

_____

_____

_____

Copyright © by Holt, Rinehart and Winston. All rights reserved.

CHAPTER

5 VOCABULARY REVIEW WORKSHEET

Vocabulary Garden

After you finish Chapter 5, give this puzzle a try!

Write the word or phrase being described below in the appropriate space on the next page.

1. chromosomes with matching information

2. carry genes that determine the sex of offspring

3. the two genes that govern the same characteristic

4. an organism's inherited combination of alleles

5. nuclear division in eukaryotic cells in which each cell receives a copy of the original chromosomes

6. the passing of traits from parents to offspring

7. cell division that produces sex cells

8. kind of trait that seemed to vanish in the offspring produced in Mendel's first experiment

9. tool used to visualize all the possible combinations of alleles from parents

10. kind of trait that always appeared in the offspring produced in Mendel's first experiment

11. A true-_____ plant always produces offspring with the same trait as the parent(s).

12. A self-_____ plant contains both male and female reproductive structures.

13. male sex cells

14. an organism's inherited appearance

15. female sex cells

16. the mathematical chance that an event will occur

17. located on chromosomes and carry hereditary instructions

Copyright © by Holt, Rinehart and Winston. All rights reserved.

Vocabulary Garden, continued

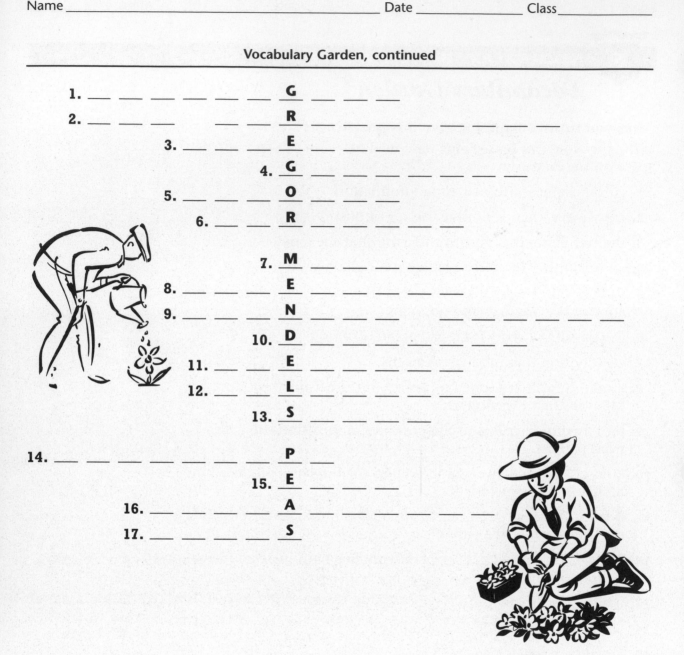

1. __ __ __ __ __ __ **G** __ __ __
2. __ __ __ __ __ **R** __ __ __ __ __ __ __ __ __
3. __ __ __ __ **E** __ __ __ __ __
4. __ __ __ **G** __ __ __ __ __
5. __ __ __ **O** __ __ __ __
6. __ __ __ __ **R**
7. **M** __ __ __
8. __ __ __ __ **E** __ __ __ __
9. __ __ __ __ **N** __ __ __ __ __ __ __ __
10. __ **D** __ __ __ __ __ __
11. __ __ __ **E** __ __ __
12. __ __ __ **L** __ __ __
13. __ __ **S** __ __ __
14. __ __ __ __ __ **P** __ __ __
15. __ __ __ **E** __ __ __
16. __ __ __ **A** __ __ __ __ __
17. __ __ __ __ **S**

18. What do Gregor Mendel's peas have to do with the study of heredity?

_____

_____

_____

_____

_____

_____

Copyright © by Holt, Rinehart and Winston. All rights reserved.

DNA Mutations

Complete this worksheet after reading Chapter 6, Section 2.

DNA is made up of nucleotides that each contain a sugar, a phosphate, and a base. The four possible bases are: adenine, cytosine, thymine, and guanine. Remember that adenine and thymine are complementary and form pairs, and cytosine and guanine are complementary and form pairs.

1. Below is half of a section of DNA that has been split apart and is ready to copy itself. Write the appropriate letter in the space provided to build the DNA's new complementary strand.

G - - - - - - - - - - ___

T - - - - - - - - - ___

A - - - - - - - - - ___

A - - - - - - - - - ___

C - - - - - - - - - ___

T - - - - - - - - - ___

C - - - - - - - - - ___

C - - - - - - - - - ___

T - - - - - - - - - ___

2. Sometimes mistakes happen when the DNA is being copied. These mistakes, or mutations, change the order of the bases in DNA. There are three kinds of mutations that can occur in DNA: deletion, insertion, and substitution.

   a. Below are two sequences—an original sequence of bases in DNA and the sequence of bases after a mutation has occurred. On the original base sequence, show where the mutation has occurred by circling the appropriate base pair, and write what type of mutation it is in the space provided.

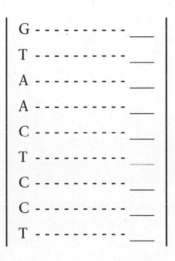

C G	C G
T A	T A
C G	C G
C G	C G
T A	T A
A T	A T
A T	A T
A T	A T
C G	T A
C G	C G
T A	T A

Base sequence in   Base sequence in a cell
original cell DNA   with mutated DNA

_____

Copyright © by Holt, Rinehart and Winston. All rights reserved.

b. Below are two more sequences—an original sequence of bases in DNA and the sequence of bases after a mutation has occurred. On the original base sequence, show where the mutation has occurred by circling the appropriate base pair, and write what type of mutation it is in the space provided.

C	G		C	G
T	A		T	A
A	T		A	T
C	G		C	G
C	G		C	G
G	C		G	C
T	A		T	A
A	T		A	T
A	T		A	T
G	C		A	T
A	T		T	A
T	A			

Base sequence in   Base sequence in a cell
original cell DNA   with mutated DNA

3. Ribosomes "read" a complementary copy of DNA in order to make proteins. Each group of three bases forms the code for an amino acid. When mutations occur in DNA, they can change the information that the DNA carries.

To understand this process better, look at the sentence below, which uses only three-letter words.

AMY GOT THE RED HOT POT OFF THE LOG

If one letter is deleted from this sentence, it can become:

AMY GTT HER EDH OTP OTO FFT HEL OG

How is this similar to what can happen when a mutation occurs in DNA?

_____

_____

_____

_____

Copyright © by Holt, Rinehart and Winston. All rights reserved.

Name _____ Date _____ Class _____

Unraveling Genes

Try this puzzle after you finish reading Chapter 6!

Solve the clues and unscramble the letters to fill in the blanks. Fill the letters in the squares and read the final clue to unravel the secret message.

1. Molecule that carries our hereditary information: NAD

___ ___ ___
  11

2. Subunits of DNA: DISTONEUCLE

___ ___ ___ ___ ___ ___ ___ ___ ___ ___
                                    1

3. Nucleotide base known as A: ENIDANE

___ ___ ___ ___ ___ ___ ___
 16   14

4. Complement of question 3: TIEHYMN

___ ___ ___ ___ ___ ___ ___
        5

5. Nucleotide base known as G: NUANIGE

___ ___ ___ ___ ___ ___ ___
              15

6. Complement of question 5: YOSTINCE

___ ___ ___ ___ ___ ___ ___ ___
          4

7. Shape of a DNA molecule (two words): EXELLIDOBUH

___ ___ ___ ___ ___ ___ ___   ___ ___ ___ ___
    12   7

8. Organelle that manufactures proteins: MOOSERIB

___ ___ ___ ___ ___ ___ ___ ___
                      10

9. A change in the order of the bases of an organism's DNA: UNMATIOT

___ ___ ___ ___ ___ ___ ___ ___
 13   17

10. Anything that can cause damage to DNA: UNGATEM

___ ___ ___ ___ ___ ___ ___
        9

11. A tool for tracing a trait through generations of a family: DEEPGIRE

___ ___ ___ ___ ___ ___ ___ ___
 6

12. Manipulation of genes that allows scientists to put genes from one organism into another organism: (two words) NEETIEGGINGECINNER

___ ___ ___ ___ ___ ___ ___ ___ ___
              18

___ ___ ___ ___ ___ ___ ___ ___ ___ ___

Copyright © by Holt, Rinehart and Winston. All rights reserved.

Unraveling Genes, continued

13. Analysis of fragments of DNA as a form of identification (two words):
PANDINGINGFRENRIT

___ ___ ___   ___ ___ ___ ___ ___ ___ ___ ___ ___ ___ ___ ___ ___ ___ ___
                        19

14. Genes are located on these structures that are found in the nucleus of most cells:
SHROCOMEMOS

___ ___ ___ ___ ___ ___ ___ ___ ___ ___ ___ ___
                                    8

15. When organisms with certain desirable traits are mated: SGEEDETRINELCVIEB

___ ___ ___ ___ ___ ___ ___ ___ ___   ___ ___ ___ ___ ___ ___ ___ ___ ___
        3

16. Genetic engineering is used to repair damaged: NEGSE

___ ___ ___ ___ ___
        2

FINAL CLUE:

Occurs when different traits are equally dominant and each allele has its own degree of influence:

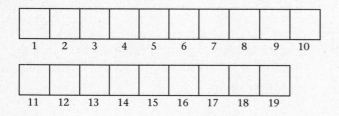

Copyright © by Holt, Rinehart and Winston. All rights reserved.

CHAPTER

7 **REINFORCEMENT WORKSHEET**

Bicentennial Celebration

Complete this worksheet after reading Chapter 7, Section 2.

Imagine that it is 2059—the 200th anniversary of the publication of Darwin's *On the Origin of Species*. You are a reporter for a science magazine that is publishing a special issue about evolutionary biology. Your assignment is to write an article about Darwin, his travels, and his scientific theory of evolution. Include details about the Galápagos finches and how Darwin first got the idea for his theory, and explain the steps in the process of natural selection. Don't forget to give your article an eye-catching headline!

_____

_____

_____

_____

_____

_____

_____

_____

_____

_____

_____

_____

_____

_____

_____

_____

Copyright © by Holt, Rinehart and Winston. All rights reserved.

Name _____ Date _____ Class_____

VOCABULARY REVIEW WORKSHEET

Charles Darwin's Legacy

After you finish Chapter 7, give this puzzle a try.
Unscramble each of the words below, and write the word in the space provided.

1. SISEPCE — a group of organisms that can mate to produce fertile offspring

2. CATEISPOIN — the process by which two populations become so different they can no longer interbreed

3. ASTRIT — distinguishing qualities that can be passed on from parents to offspring

4. SVELETICE — _____ breeding is the breeding of organisms that have a certain desired trait.

5. TAPATIDONA — a hereditary characteristic that helps an organism survive and reproduce in its environment

6. ALTRAUN — Successful reproduction is the fourth step of _____ selection.

7. GLEVITIAS — describes once-useful structures

8. SLOSFIS — solidified remains of once-living organisms

9. MAUTONTI — a change in a gene at the DNA level

Now unscramble the circled letters to find Darwin's legacy.

Copyright © by Holt, Rinehart and Winston. All rights reserved.

CHAPTER

8 **REINFORCEMENT WORKSHEET**

Earth Timeline

Complete this worksheet after you finish reading Chapter 8, Section 1.
Scientists use four major divisions to talk about the Earth's history:
Precambrian time, the Paleozoic era, the Mesozoic era, and the
Cenozoic era. Precambrian time lasted for about 88 percent of the
4.6 billion years of Earth's history. The Paleozoic era was about
6.3 percent of Earth's history. The Mesozoic era was about 4.0 percent
of Earth's history. The Cenozoic era has lasted for about 1.4 percent
of the Earth's history.

The Earth's history is difficult to imagine because it is so long. But
what if the entire history of the Earth could fit into a single human
life span of 80 years? Fill in the timeline below to show how old a
person would be when each era begins. If the first single-celled
organism appeared 3.5 billion years ago, how old would the person
be when the first single-celled organism appears on Earth? Indicate
this on the timeline.

Age in years

```
 0 ─
 5 ─
10 ─
15 ─
20 ─
25 ─
30 ─
35 ─
40 ─
45 ─
50 ─
55 ─
60 ─
65 ─
70 ─
75 ─
80 ─
```

Copyright © by Holt, Rinehart and Winston. All rights reserved.

CHAPTER

8 **REINFORCEMENT WORKSHEET**

Condensed History

Complete this worksheet after you finish reading Chapter 8, Section 2.
Many important events that have occurred since the Earth was formed are listed below.
Fill in the diagram below, listing the events in chronological order.

Prokaryotes form.

Cells with nuclei form.

Began 65 million years ago

First birds appear.

Large mammals appear.

The ozone layer develops.

Dinosaurs dominate the Earth.

Plants become established on land.

Humans appear.

Crawling insects appear on land.

Many reptile species evolve.

Organisms suffer largest mass extinction known.

Small mammals survive mass extinction.

Began 540 million years ago

Cyanobacteria begin photosynthesis and produce oxygen.

Began 4.6 billion years ago

Winged insects appear.

Began 248 million years ago

Precambrian Time
Paleozoic Era
Mesozoic Era
Cenozoic Era

Copyright © by Holt, Rinehart and Winston. All rights reserved.

CHAPTER

8   VOCABULARY REVIEW WORKSHEET

Mary Leakey's Search

Try this puzzle after you finish Chapter 8.
Solve each of the clues below, and write your answer in the spaces provided. Then complete the quotation by Mary Leakey on the next page by writing the letter that corresponds to each number in the empty boxes.

1. large mammals evolved during this era.

___ ___ ___ ___ ___ ___
        5   6

2. scientist who uses fossils to reconstruct what happened in Earth's history

___ ___ ___ ___ ___ ___ ___ ___ ___ ___ ___ ___
          8   10   33 31

3. measuring the ratio of unstable to stable atoms in a rock sample to determine the age of the fossil it contains

___ ___ ___ ___ ___ ___ ___ ___ ___ ___ ___ ___
24 52   28   23   17   48

4. the first true cells

___ ___ ___ ___ ___ ___ ___ ___ ___
      4   1 35   53

5. cells that contain a nucleus

___ ___ ___ ___ ___ ___ ___ ___ ___
  9 30   42 56

6. scientist who discovered fossilized footprints in Tanzania

___ ___ ___ ___ ___ ___ ___ ___ ___
    13   41   54   7

7. hominid that lived in Germany 230,000 years ago

___ ___ ___ ___ ___ ___ ___ ___
16   37   51

8. an imprint of a living thing preserved in rock

___ ___ ___ ___ ___ ___
14   12

9. Lucy is the most complete example of a(n) _____ ever found.

___ ___ ___ ___ ___ ___ ___ ___ ___
 3   36   18   32

10. When a species dies out completely, it becomes _____ .

___ ___ ___ ___ ___
38   15   20

11. the theory that explains how the continents move

___ ___ ___ ___ ___ ___ ___ ___
27   50   47   11

Copyright © by Holt, Rinehart and Winston. All rights reserved.

12. a group of mammals with binocular vision

— $\underset{49}{—}$ — — — $\underset{45}{—}$ — —

13. Humans and their humanlike ancestors are called _____ .

$\underset{46}{—}$ — — — $\underset{55}{—}$ — — —

14. organisms that don't need oxygen to survive

— — $\underset{39}{—}$ — $\underset{25}{—}$ — — —

15. a gas that absorbs ultraviolet radiation

$\underset{2}{—}$ — — $\underset{57}{—}$ —

16. the single landmass that existed about 245 million years ago

— $\underset{19}{—}$ — — — $\underset{26}{—}$ —

17. The first birds appeared during this era.

— — — $\underset{29}{—}$ — — $\underset{43}{—}$ —

18. During this era, the first land-dwelling organisms appeared.

— $\underset{40}{—}$ — $\underset{22}{—}$ — — —

19. Cyanobacteria produce this gas during photosynthesis.

— — $\underset{21}{—}$ — — —

20. the time it takes for half of the unstable atoms in a sample to decay

— — — $\underset{34}{—}$ – — — $\underset{44}{—}$ —

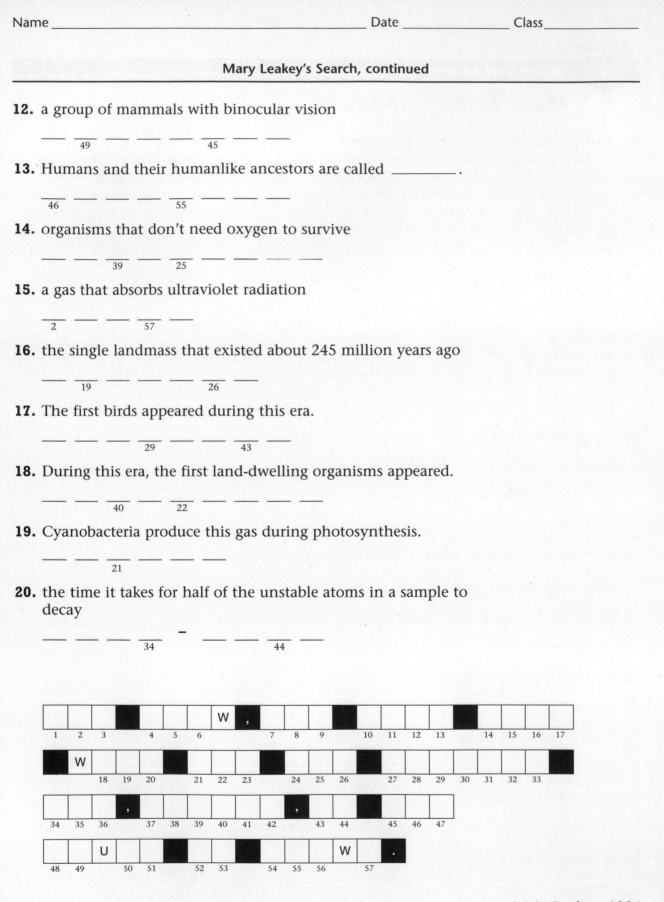

— Mary Leakey, 1994

Copyright © by Holt, Rinehart and Winston. All rights reserved.

Name _____ Date _____ Class _____

Keys to the Kingdom

Complete this worksheet after you have finished reading Chapter 9, Section 2.

Patty dropped her notes while she was studying the six kingdoms of living things, and now she isn't sure which facts belong to which kingdom. Each of the six boxes on the next page is labeled with the name of one of the kingdoms. Help Patty out by listing the facts, descriptions, and examples from Patty's notes below in the appropriate boxes. Be careful—some notes may fit in more than one kingdom.

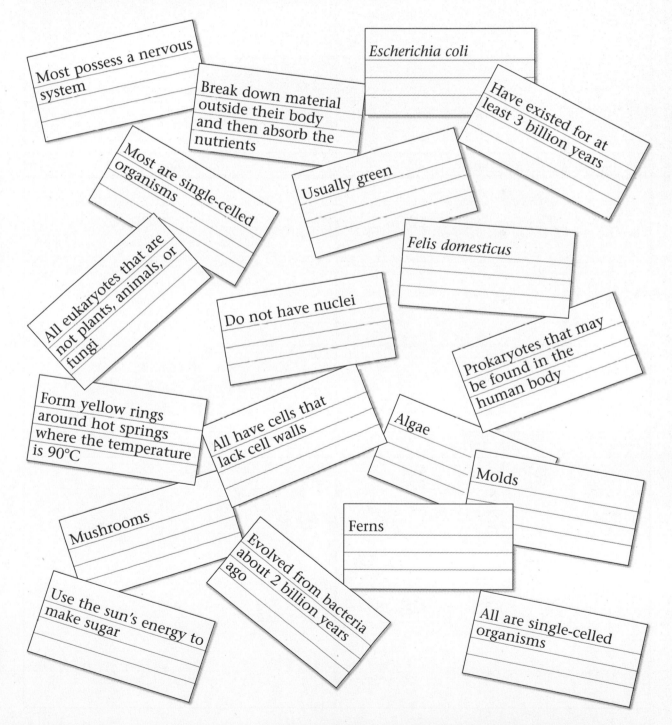

Most possess a nervous system

Break down material outside their body and then absorb the nutrients

Escherichia coli

Have existed for at least 3 billion years

Most are single-celled organisms

Usually green

Felis domesticus

All eukaryotes that are not plants, animals, or fungi

Do not have nuclei

Prokaryotes that may be found in the human body

Form yellow rings around hot springs where the temperature is 90°C

All have cells that lack cell walls

Algae

Molds

Mushrooms

Ferns

Evolved from bacteria about 2 billion years ago

Use the sun's energy to make sugar

All are single-celled organisms

Copyright © by Holt, Rinehart and Winston. All rights reserved.

Animalia	Plantae

Protista	Fungi

Eubacteria	Archaebacteria

Copyright © by Holt, Rinehart and Winston. All rights reserved.

CHAPTER

9 VOCABULARY REVIEW WORKSHEET

Classification Clues

Complete this puzzle after you have finished Chapter 9.

Solve the clues to see what words are hidden in the puzzle. Words in the puzzle are hidden vertically, horizontally, and diagonally.

1. List the seven levels used by scientists to classify organisms in order from most general to least general.

a. _____

b. _____

c. _____

d. _____

e. _____

f. _____

g. _____

2. For each of the following descriptions, write the kingdom of the organisms being described in the space provided.

a. _____ Single-celled organisms without nuclei, such as *Escherichia coli,* which live in the human body

b. _____ Multicellular, eukaryotic organisms that are usually green and make sugar through photosynthesis

c. _____ Unicellular prokaryotes that have been on Earth for at least 3 billion years

d. _____ Multicellular organisms whose cells have nuclei but do not have cell walls

e. _____ Multicellular organisms that have cells containing nuclei and that absorb nutrients from their surroundings after breaking them down with digestive juices

f. _____ Single-celled or multicellular, eukaryotic organisms that are not plants, animals, or fungi

3. Linnaeus founded _____, the science of identifying, naming, and classifying living things.

4. A _____ key is a special guide used to identify unknown organisms.

Copyright © by Holt, Rinehart and Winston. All rights reserved.

Classification Clues, continued

A	O	D	R	P	H	Y	L	U	M	X	O	B	K
M	R	I	O	K	N	A	R	I	P	P	H	Y	Y
O	E	C	M	R	E	H	O	C	M	L	Y	M	T
D	R	H	H	O	D	F	N	S	I	A	O	D	C
G	A	O	I	A	G	E	S	C	A	N	M	S	L
N	L	T	K	B	E	U	R	T	O	T	S	P	E
I	Q	O	I	U	N	B	E	X	S	A	U	E	U
K	H	M	Y	L	U	T	A	D	L	E	E	C	G
P	R	O	T	I	S	T	A	C	P	S	A	I	S
A	Y	U	T	I	E	B	D	R	T	E	R	E	F
I	L	S	G	U	V	O	G	U	C	E	H	S	O
Z	U	N	A	E	U	B	A	C	T	E	R	I	A
M	U	G	T	F	N	W	P	L	R	B	S	I	Y
F	A	M	I	L	Y	A	N	I	M	A	L	I	A

Copyright © by Holt, Rinehart and Winston. All rights reserved.

Name _____ Date _____ Class _____

Bacteria Bonanza

Complete this worksheet after you finish reading Chapter 10, Section 1.

Complete the outline below using the following terms: *spirilla, photosynthetic, methane makers, eubacteria, decomposers, bacilli, heat lovers, consumers, salt lovers, producers, archaebacteria, parasites, cyanobacteria,* and *cocci.*

Bacteria

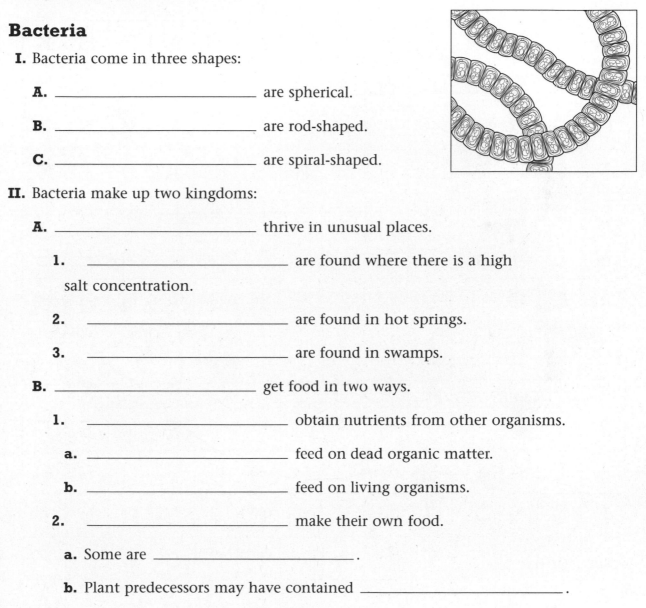

I. Bacteria come in three shapes:

   A. _____ are spherical.

   B. _____ are rod-shaped.

   C. _____ are spiral-shaped.

II. Bacteria make up two kingdoms:

   A. _____ thrive in unusual places.

     1. _____ are found where there is a high salt concentration.

     2. _____ are found in hot springs.

     3. _____ are found in swamps.

   B. _____ get food in two ways.

     1. _____ obtain nutrients from other organisms.

       a. _____ feed on dead organic matter.

       b. _____ feed on living organisms.

     2. _____ make their own food.

       a. Some are _____ .

       b. Plant predecessors may have contained _____ .

Copyright © by Holt, Rinehart and Winston. All rights reserved.

The Lytic Cycle

Complete this worksheet after you finish reading Chapter 10, Section 3.

The figure below shows the steps of the lytic cycle. At the bottom of the page are descriptions of each of the steps in the figure. Choose the description that best matches the step in the diagram, and write the letter that corresponds to each step on the blank provided. Not all descriptions will be used.

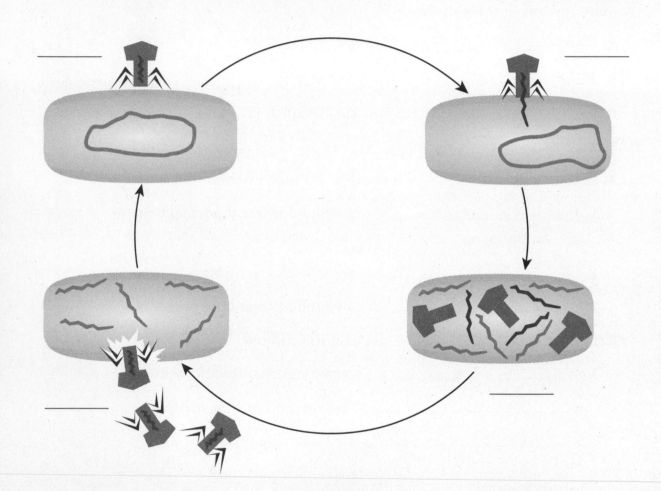

Copyright © by Holt, Rinehart and Winston. All rights reserved.

Descriptions

A. The host cell undergoes cell division, producing new cells that each contain a copy of the virus's genes.

B. The new viruses burst out of the host cell, destroying the host cell.

C. The virus's genes turn the host cell into a virus factory.

D. The virus remains inactive for a long period of time.

E. The virus attaches itself to the host cell.

F. The virus enters the cell, or genetic material of the virus is injected into the host cell.

Copyright © by Holt, Rinehart and Winston. All rights reserved.

CHAPTER
10 **VOCABULARY REVIEW WORKSHEET**

A Puzzle of Tiny Things

After you finish reading Chapter 10, give this puzzle a try!

Use the clues below to fill in the crossword puzzle on the next page.

ACROSS

5. type of bacteria that consume nitrogen in the air and change it into a form plants can use

10. bacteria that invade a host organism and obtain nutrients from the host's cells

12. a cell that lacks a nucleus

13. medicines used to kill bacteria and other microorganisms

14. a solution containing a weakened or inactive version of a virus

16. the use of bacteria and other microorganisms to change pollutants in soil and water into harmless chemicals

DOWN

1. the cycle of infection in which more viruses are produced and the host cell is destroyed

2. bacteria that remain inactive until environmental conditions are favorable

3. an organism that supports a parasite

4. a microscopic particle that invades a cell and often destroys it

6. one type of simple cell division that bacteria use to reproduce; binary _____

7. organism that gets energy by breaking down the remains of dead organisms

8. spherical-shaped bacteria

9. long, spiral-shaped bacteria

11. type of bacteria that digest the milk sugar lactose

15. organism that obtains its food from other organisms

A Puzzle of Tiny Things, continued

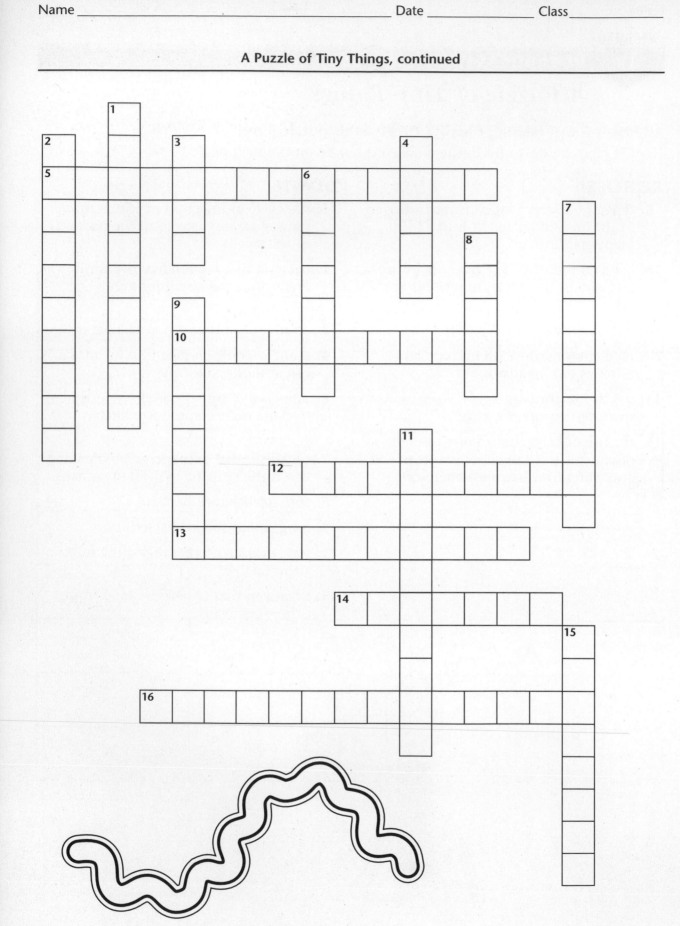

Copyright © by Holt, Rinehart and Winston. All rights reserved.

CHAPTER

11 REINFORCEMENT WORKSHEET

Protists on Parade

Complete the table below after you finish reading Chapter 11, Section 1.

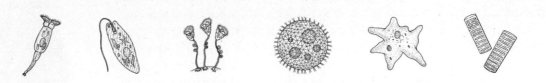

Term	Definition	Example
Parasite		"late blight"
	makes its own food, usually by photosynthesis	
Consumer		scrambled egg slime mold
Flagella		
Cilia		
Pseudopodia		amoeba
Spore-forming		
	reproduction in which two organisms join together and exchange genetic material	
Fission		euglena

Copyright © by Holt, Rinehart and Winston. All rights reserved.

An Ode to a Fungus

Complete this worksheet after you finish reading Chapter 11, Section 2.

A science magazine has asked your friend, the well-known poet Madeline Molde, to write a poem about fungi. Madeline started her poem, but now she has writers' block. The poem is unfinished and her deadline is tomorrow! The poem needs to be at least 12 lines long (but it can be longer) and should contain factual information about fungi. Use the terms in Chapter 11 to help Madeline finish her poem!

Fungi
Beautiful, black, fuzzy mold!
You grow in my fridge on food that is old.
Fungi! Yummy truffles that I love to eat,

_____

_____

_____

_____

_____

_____

_____

_____

_____

_____

_____

_____

_____

_____

_____

_____

Copyright © by Holt, Rinehart and Winston. All rights reserved.

Name _____ Date _____ Class _____

A Moldy Puzzle

After you finish reading Chapter 11, give this puzzle a try!

Fill in the blanks with the appropriate terms, and then use the terms to complete the puzzle on the next page.

1. An organism that invades the body of another organism is a

   _____ .

2. _____ are fungi that do not fit into other standard groups of fungi.

3. _____ are animal-like protists that are single-celled consumers.

4. Plantlike protists that convert the sun's energy into food through photosynthesis are

   called _____ .

5. The organism that is harmed by a parasite is called the

   _____ .

6. A _____ is made of a fungus and an alga that grow intertwined.

7. Any eukaryotic organism that is part of the kingdom Protista is called a

   _____ .

8. _____ -like fungi include black bread mold.

9. Amoebas use _____ , or "false feet," to move around.

10. _____ are chains of cells that make up multicellular fungi.

11. The group of fungi that includes umbrella-shaped mushrooms and puffballs is called

    _____ .

12. A protist that obtains its food from dead organic matter or from the body of

    another organism is called a _____ protist.

13. A _____ is a small reproductive cell protected by a thick cell wall.

14. Fungi that reproduce by spores that develop in an ascus are called

    _____ .

15. Kingdom _____ includes complex, multicellular organisms that obtain food by breaking down other substances in their surroundings and absorbing the nutrients.

16. The major part of a multicellular fungus is a twisted mass of hyphae that have grown

    together called a _____ .

17. A shapeless, fuzzy fungus is a _____ .

18. _____ are single-celled, microscopic, photosynthetic organisms that float near the surface of the ocean.

Copyright © by Holt, Rinehart and Winston. All rights reserved.

A Moldy Puzzle, continued

Search the puzzle below to find each of the terms you wrote in the blanks on the previous page, and circle these terms in the puzzle. Words may appear horizontally, vertically, backward, or diagonally.

S	M	O	M	E	T	H	R	E	A	D	O	V	E	P
R	U	R	H	O	S	T	H	E	T	A	C	I	S	I
N	I	B	O	W	I	B	L	J	E	B	L	E	I	M
I	L	R	D	S	M	S	P	O	R	E	U	F	L	P
I	E	Y	T	H	O	A	H	E	R	D	B	E	S	E
G	C	A	L	A	R	N	Y	W	O	T	F	H	A	R
N	Y	T	I	A	P	H	T	P	E	A	U	R	D	F
U	M	O	S	F	E	O	O	H	N	C	N	E	I	E
F	N	I	P	N	K	D	P	A	Y	L	G	U	L	C
L	T	A	R	B	I	Y	L	D	O	P	I	R	O	T
E	T	H	O	A	L	Y	A	L	I	C	H	E	N	F
P	R	O	T	I	S	T	N	T	H	I	N	A	K	U
S	D	L	O	M	U	S	K	H	E	I	S	L	E	N
N	O	T	Z	A	G	N	T	F	L	U	N	G	I	G
I	N	K	O	A	N	N	O	S	A	S	A	A	N	I
Y	M	O	A	R	U	E	N	S	O	D	O	E	E	S
T	H	S	A	C	F	U	N	G	I	E	L	I	O	N

Copyright © by Holt, Rinehart and Winston. All rights reserved.

Name _____ Date _____ Class _____

Classifying Plants

Complete this worksheet after you finish reading Chapter 12, Section 3.

Each of the boxes below represents one of the main groups of living plants. Write the descriptions given at the bottom of the page in the appropriate box. Some descriptions may be used more than once.

Nonvascular plants	Vascular plants without seeds
Vascular plants with seeds but without flowers	**Vascular plants with seeds and flowers**

Notes

- ancestors grew very large
- conifers are an example
- provide land animals with almost all of the food they need to survive
- include the oldest living trees on Earth
- have rhizoids instead of roots

- angiosperms
- seeds are surrounded by a fruit
- are the most successful group of plants today
- mosses and liverworts
- usually the first plants to inhabit a new environment
- formed fossil fuels

- ferns, horsetails, and club mosses
- gymnosperms
- must obtain water by osmosis
- contain xylem and phloem to transport water and food
- seeds develop in a cone or on fleshy structures attached to branches

Copyright © by Holt, Rinehart and Winston. All rights reserved.

CHAPTER

12 **REINFORCEMENT WORKSHEET**

Drawing Dicots

Complete this worksheet after you finish reading Chapter 12, Section 3.

There are two classes of angiosperms—monocots and dicots. The main difference between the two classes is that monocots have one seed leaf and dicots have two seed leaves. However, there are other differences between them.

Below are illustrations of some of the features that distinguish monocots from dicots. Use the description of how a dicot differs from a monocot to draw the same features for a dicot.

Monocot	How is a dicot different from a monocot?	Dicot
Arrangement of vascular tissue	A monocot has bundles of vascular tissue scattered throughout the stem, while a dicot has bundles of vascular tissue arranged in a ring.	Arrangement of vascular tissue
Flower	A monocot has a flower with parts in threes, while a dicot has a flower with parts in fours or fives.	Flower
Pattern of leaf vein	A monocot has leaves with parallel veins, while a dicot has leaves with branching veins.	Pattern of leaf vein

Copyright © by Holt, Rinehart and Winston. All rights reserved.

CHAPTER
12 **VOCABULARY REVIEW WORKSHEET**

Those Puzzling Plants

After finishing Chapter 12, give this puzzle a try!

Solve each of the clues below, and write your answer in the spaces provided.

1. spore-producing stage of a plant

__ __ __ __ __ __ __ __ __ __
                         24

2. plants with specialized tissue to move materials from one part of the plant to another

__ __ __ __ __ __ __ __ __
     3

3. male reproductive structure in a flower

__ __ __ __ __ __ __
      12

4. dustlike particles produced in the anthers of flowers

__ __ __ __ __ __
      19

5. small, hairlike threads of cells that keep mosses grounded

__ __ __ __ __ __ __ __
        14

6. openings in the epidermis of a leaf that let CO_2 into the leaves

__ __ __ __ __ __ __
      20

7. plant "pipes" that transport sugar molecules

__ __ __ __ __ __
    2

8. waxy layer that coats the surface of stems and leaves

__ __ __ __ __ __ __
      18

9. structures that cover immature flowers

__ __ __ __ __ __
 5   26

10. usually obtains water close to the soil surface

__ __ __ __ __ __ __ __ __ __ __
    25   9

11. nonflowering, seed-producing plants

__ __ __ __ __ __ __ __ __ __
         8

12. part of a flower that contains the ovules

__ __ __ __ __ __
   1

Copyright © by Holt, Rinehart and Winston. All rights reserved.

13. seed leaf inside a seed

— — — — — — $\frac{}{11}$ — $\frac{}{13}$

14. attract pollinators to the flower

— — — $\frac{}{22}$ — — —

15. outermost layer of cells that covers roots, stems, leaves, and flower parts

— — — — $\frac{}{7}$ — — — —

16. plants that have no "pipes" to transport materials from one part of the plant to another

— — — $\frac{}{15}$ — — — $\frac{}{27}$ — — —

17. seed-producing plants with flowers

— — — — — — — $\frac{}{23}$ — —

18. plant "pipes" that transport water and minerals

— — — $\frac{}{10}$ —

19. can obtain water that is deep underground

— — — — $\frac{}{17}$ — —

20. plant stage that produces sex cells

— $\frac{}{6}$ — $\frac{}{28}$ — — — — — — —

21. tip of the pistil; collects pollen

$\frac{}{21}$ — — — — —

22. underground stem of a fern

— — — — — — $\frac{}{4}$

23. female reproductive structure in a flower

— — — — $\frac{}{16}$ —

Write the letter that corresponds to each number in the empty boxes
to form the beginning of a well-known poem.

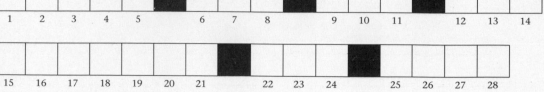

Copyright © by Holt, Rinehart and Winston. All rights reserved.

CHAPTER

13 **REINFORCEMENT WORKSHEET**

Fertilizing Flowers

Complete this worksheet after you finish reading Chapter 13, Section 1.

Flowers are adaptations that plants use for sexual reproduction.

1. Below is a cross section of a flower. Label the parts of the flower by writing each of the terms in the appropriate space.

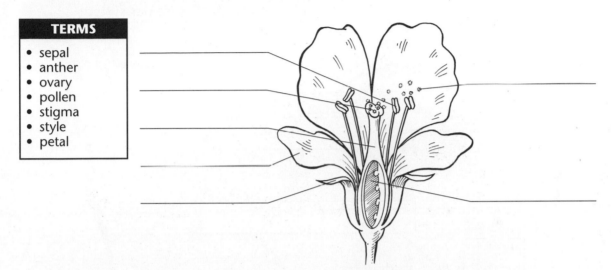

TERMS

- sepal
- anther
- ovary
- pollen
- stigma
- style
- petal

2. For fertilization to occur, a sperm has to reach the egg. Use the terms in the box below to label the following illustration, which shows how a sperm cell fuses with an egg in a flower.

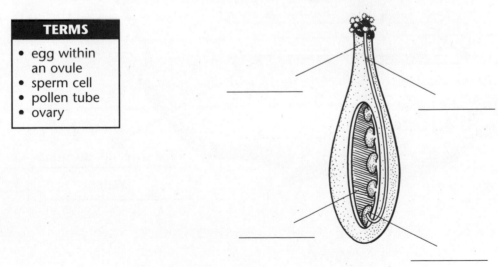

TERMS

- egg within an ovule
- sperm cell
- pollen tube
- ovary

3. In the illustration above, which structure turns into the fruit after fertilization?

_____

_____

Copyright © by Holt, Rinehart and Winston. All rights reserved.

A Leaf's Work Is Never Done

Complete this worksheet after you finish reading Chapter 13, Section 2.

A plant makes food in its leaves. Complete the outline below by filling in the blanks in the diagram with the words at the bottom of the page.

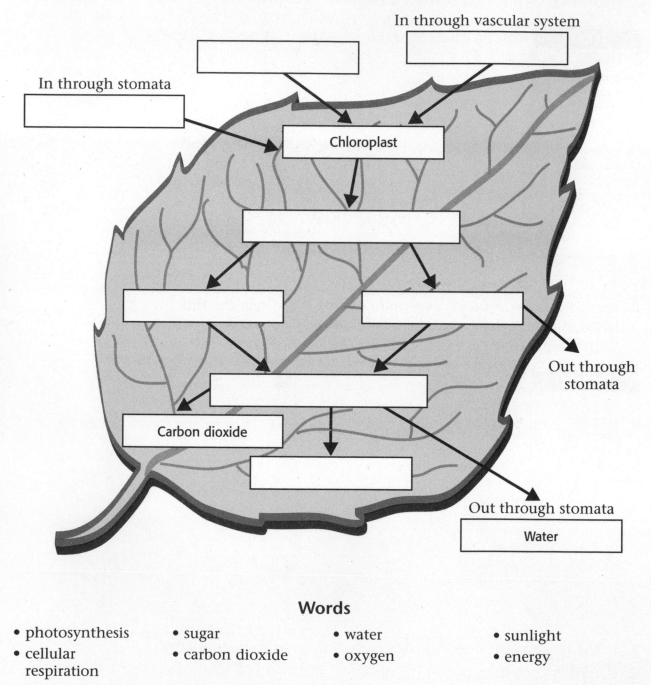

In through vascular system

In through stomata

Chloroplast

Out through stomata

Out through stomata

Carbon dioxide

Water

Words

- photosynthesis
- cellular respiration
- sugar
- carbon dioxide
- water
- oxygen
- sunlight
- energy

Copyright © by Holt, Rinehart and Winston. All rights reserved.

How Plants Respond to Change

Complete this worksheet after you finish reading Chapter 13, Section 3.

Although plants don't walk and talk, they do respond to stimuli in their environment. Plants respond to stimuli by growing in a particular direction. Plant growth away from a stimulus is a negative tropism. Plant growth toward a stimulus is a positive tropism.

1. The plant shown below has just been moved next to a window from a room with no direct light. Sketch what the plant will look like in a few days.

In a few days

2. Phototropism is a change in the growth of a plant in response to light. Is phototropism positive or negative?

_____

3. The plant shown below has just been tipped over on its side. Sketch what the plant will look like in a few days. (Hint: The plant will respond to gravity.)

In a few days

4. Gravitropism is a change in the direction of the growth of a plant in response to gravity. Is gravitropism of most shoot tips positive or negative?

_____

Copyright © by Holt, Rinehart and Winston. All rights reserved.

CHAPTER
13 **VOCABULARY REVIEW WORKSHEET**

Scrambled Plants

After you finish Chapter 13, try this puzzle!

Use the clues to unscramble each of the words below, and write the word in the space provided.

1. IOSDDUUEC — a tree that loses all of its leaves at the same time each year

2. TAOTSMA — the openings in a leaf's epidermis that allow carbon dioxide in and oxygen and water out

3. OISRMTP — a change in a plant's growth in response to a stimulus

4. NEREGEVER — a tree that keeps its leaves year-round

5. PROLYHCHOLL — a green pigment that absorbs light energy

6. VAPMTGROSIIR — a change in the direction a plant grows in response to gravity

7. MOPTOPSIRHOT — a change in the way a plant grows in response to light

8. EUALCRLL EAPRRIINOST (two words) — the process that converts the energy stored in food into a form cells can use

9. AAIINNTTRRSPO — the loss of water from leaves

10. TRODNAM — inactive state of a seed

Now unscramble the circled letters to find the organelle that contains the photosynthetic pigment in plants.

Copyright © by Holt, Rinehart and Winston. All rights reserved.

50 HOLT SCIENCE AND TECHNOLOGY

CHAPTER
14 **REINFORCEMENT WORKSHEET**

What Makes an Animal an Animal?

Complete this worksheet after reading Chapter 14, Section 1.

Whales, armadillos, hummingbirds, spiders… animals come in all shapes and sizes. Not all animals have backbones, and not all animals have hair. So what makes an animal an animal?

Complete the chart below by using the words and phrases at the bottom of the page.

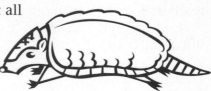

Animal Characteristics

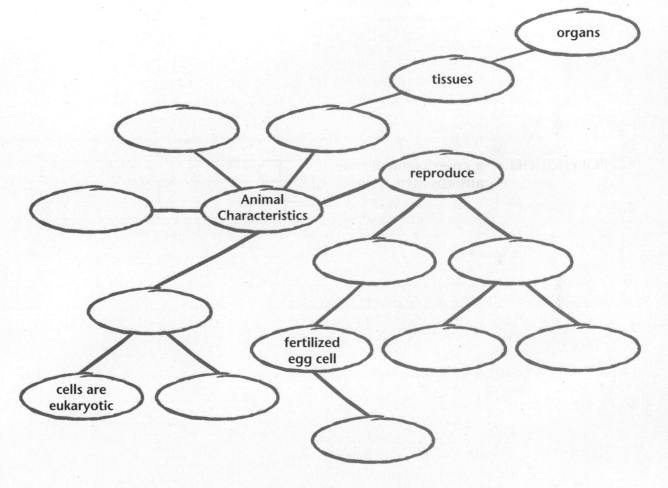

Words and Phrases

- move
- budding
- develop from embryos
- have specialized parts
- sexually

- asexually
- multicellular
- cells have no cell walls
- division
- are consumers

Copyright © by Holt, Rinehart and Winston. All rights reserved.

Animal Interviews

Complete this worksheet after reading Chapter 14, Section 2.

Imagine that you work with Dr. Phishtof Finz, a researcher who can really talk to the animals. Below are some sections of his taped animal interviews. Your job is to decide what animal behavior or characteristic is being described and to write it in the space provided. Possible answers are *warning coloration, migration, hibernation, estivation,* and *camouflage.*

Interviewed animal		**Behavior or characteristic**
Canada goose:	During the summer, we stay up in Canada. It's really a nice place in summer, with lots of food and lots of sun. But before the snow starts to fly, we high-tail it south!	_____
Arctic ground squirrel:	What's the winter like in Alaska? Strange, I really don't know. I spend all summer eating and getting my nest ready, but then during the fall I get so sleepy! I go to bed and—*poof!*—when I wake up it's spring!	_____
Desert mouse:	Oh, living in the desert is wonderful! I love sunshine. During the really hot part of the summer, of course, I stay inside my nest, and I nap a lot. It's so much cooler inside.	_____
Ladybug:	Thank you! I am a lovely shade of red, aren't I? But just between you and me, did you know that this beautiful color tells birds that I am, well, rather nasty tasting?	_____
Chameleon:	Yoo-hoo! I'm over here! See? In the potted plant. Well, yes, I am rather proud of being able to turn that particular shade of green. Not all animals can do that, you know.	_____

Copyright © by Holt, Rinehart and Winston. All rights reserved.

Puzzling Animal Behavior

After you finish reading Chapter 14, give this crossword puzzle a try!

Solve the clues below, and write the answers in the appropriate
spaces in the crossword puzzle.

ACROSS

3. to find one's way from one place to another

4. an organism that eats other organisms

6. this type of behavior can change item 17 down

7. an organism in the earliest stage of development

8. to travel from one place to another in response to the seasons or environmental conditions

10. an internal control of natural cycles

16. an area occupied by an animal or a group of animals from which other members of the species are excluded

18. this type of behavior is the interaction between animals of the same species

19. an animal that eats other animals

20. made of many cells

21. a period of inactivity that some animals experience in winter

DOWN

1. chemicals animals produce for communication

2. an animal without a backbone

5. coloration and/or texture that enables an animal to blend in with its surroundings

7. a period of reduced activity that some animals experience in summer

9. a collection of similar cells that work together to perform a specific job in the body

11. a combination of two or more of item 9 down

12. takes place when a signal travels from one animal to another and the receiver of the signal responds

13. fixed object an animal uses to find its way

14. _____ rhythms are daily cycles.

15. any animal with a skull and a backbone

17. behavior that is influenced by genes and does not depend on learning or experience

22. an animal that is eaten by another animal

Copyright © by Holt, Rinehart and Winston. All rights reserved.

Puzzling Animal Behavior, continued

Copyright © by Holt, Rinehart and Winston. All rights reserved.

Copyright © by Holt, Rinehart and Winston. All rights reserved.

CHAPTER

15 **REINFORCEMENT WORKSHEET**

Life Without a Backbone

Complete this worksheet after you finish reading Chapter 15, Section 1.

What do a butterfly, a spider, a jellyfish, a worm, a snail, an octopus, and a lobster have in common? All of these animals are invertebrates. Clearly, there are many differences between these animals. Yet the most important characteristic these animals share is something none of them have—a backbone!

Despite their obvious differences, all invertebrates share some basic characteristics. Using the list of words provided, fill in the boxes with the correct answers. There will be some words that you will not use at all.

Characteristics

spicules
asymmetry
ganglia
gut
nerve cords
bilateral symmetry
collar cells
neutron
uniform
nerve networks
radial symmetry

All About Invertebrates

An invertebrate has a body plan that can have

_____

_____

_____

An invertebrate might use these structures to digest its food.

_____

_____

An invertebrate might use one or more of the following structures to control its body movement.

_____

_____

_____

CHAPTER

15 **REINFORCEMENT WORKSHEET**

Spineless Variety

Complete this worksheet after you finish reading Chapter 15, Section 4.

In each of the four completed lists, seven phrases were accidentally placed in the wrong list. Those seven phrases describe Annelid Worms. Circle the phrases that were placed incorrectly in the complete lists, and use those phrases to complete the list for Annelid Worms.

Echinoderms

live only in the ocean
have a brain
have an endoskeleton
have a nerve ring
are covered with spines or bumps
some have a radial nerve
have a water vascular system
sand dollar
sea urchin
a bristle worm

Mollusks

live in the ocean, fresh water, or land
have open or closed circulatory system
have a foot and a mantle
usually have a shell
have a visceral mass
have complex ganglia
a leech
a clam
a snail
have segments

Annelid Worms

_____

_____

_____

_____

_____

_____

_____

Cnidarians

live in the ocean or fresh water
have a nerve cord
have a gut
have a nerve net
are in polyp or medusa form
have stinging cells
a jellyfish
a sea anemone
coral
have a closed circulatory system

Arthropods

have a well-developed brain
have jointed limbs
have a head
have an exoskeleton
have a well-developed nervous system
a tick
an earthworm
a dragonfly

Copyright © by Holt, Rinehart and Winston. All rights reserved.

CHAPTER
15 VOCABULARY REVIEW WORKSHEET

Searching for a Backbone

After you finish Chapter 15, give this puzzle a try!

Identify the word described by each clue, and write the word in the space provided. Then circle the word in the puzzle on the next page.

1. external body-support structure made of protein and chitin

   _____

2. combination of head and thorax

   _____

3. type of circulatory system in which blood is pumped through a network of vessels that form a closed loop

   _____

4. symmetry in which an organism's body has two halves that are mirror images of each other

   _____

5. groups of nerve cells

   _____

6. identical or almost identical repeating body parts

   _____

7. form of cnidarian that looks like a mushroom with tentacles

   _____

8. an animal without a backbone

   _____

9. vase-shaped form of cnidarian

   _____

10. type of circulatory system in which blood is pumped through spaces called sinuses

    _____

11. the process through which an insect develops from an egg to an adult while changing form

    _____

12. without symmetry

    _____

13. three specialized parts of arthropods formed when two or three segments grow together

    a. _____

    b. _____

    c. _____

14. symmetry in which an organism's body parts are arranged in a circle around a central point

    _____

15. eye made of many identical light-sensitive cells

    _____

16. pouch where almost all animals digest food

    _____

17. jaws found on some arthropods

    _____

Copyright © by Holt, Rinehart and Winston. All rights reserved.

Searching for a Backbone, continued

18. the space in the body where the gut is located   _____

19. an organism that feeds on another organism, usually
without killing it   _____

20. feelers that respond to touch or taste   _____

21. internal body-support structure   _____

22. organism on which the organism in item 19 lives   _____

23. system that allows echinoderms to move, eat, and
breathe   _____

M	K	D	J	P	F	B	I	L	A	T	E	R	A	L	T	A
X	E	N	D	O	S	K	E	L	E	T	O	N	P	S	K	N
F	B	T	C	O	E	L	O	M	Y	E	P	V	O	E	X	T
P	A	G	A	A	S	U	D	E	M	L	E	H	F	T	M	E
I	Q	S	H	M	Z	O	W	A	Q	V	N	X	E	I	R	N
N	V	E	Y	K	O	D	A	N	I	P	A	X	J	S	A	N
V	G	L	L	M	P	R	E	A	G	R	O	N	S	A	L	A
E	X	B	N	X	M	M	P	M	O	S	Q	L	O	R	U	E
R	D	I	A	V	O	E	D	H	K	A	W	R	Y	A	C	F
T	L	D	W	D	B	N	T	E	O	B	P	X	G	P	S	S
E	A	N	B	A	P	O	L	R	D	S	A	R	A	M	A	E
B	S	A	O	C	L	E	J	E	I	R	I	W	N	S	V	G
R	E	M	P	A	T	G	S	G	O	C	P	S	G	U	R	M
A	D	E	H	O	B	O	X	H	U	K	A	X	L	N	E	E
T	A	P	N	X	L	Q	T	N	Z	T	S	L	I	V	T	N
E	E	J	P	C	O	M	P	O	U	N	D	O	A	Z	A	T
C	H	Z	G	F	R	I	L	A	I	D	A	R	T	U	W	S

Copyright © by Holt, Rinehart and Winston. All rights reserved.

CHAPTER
16 **REINFORCEMENT WORKSHEET**

Coldblooded Critters

Complete this worksheet after you read Chapter 16, Section 4.

1. Take a look at each of the illustrations in the chart on the next page. Label each illustration "Reptiles," "Fishes," or "Amphibians."

2. Read over the characteristics listed below. Then on the next page, write each characteristic in the box next to the group of animals that commonly have that characteristic. Some characteristics may be used more than once.

thin, moist skin

ectotherms

external or internal fertilization

amniotic egg   no scales

many have scales   vertebrates

some have young born live   thick, dry skin

only internal fertilization   mostly external fertilization

fins   breathe through skin and lungs

gills   some have swim bladders

most lay eggs on land   "double life"

metamorphosis   lateral line system

eggs laid in water   breathe through lungs

some have skeletons of cartilage

many have bright colors to scare predators

almost all adults have lungs

Copyright © by Holt, Rinehart and Winston. All rights reserved.

Coldblooded Critter Chart

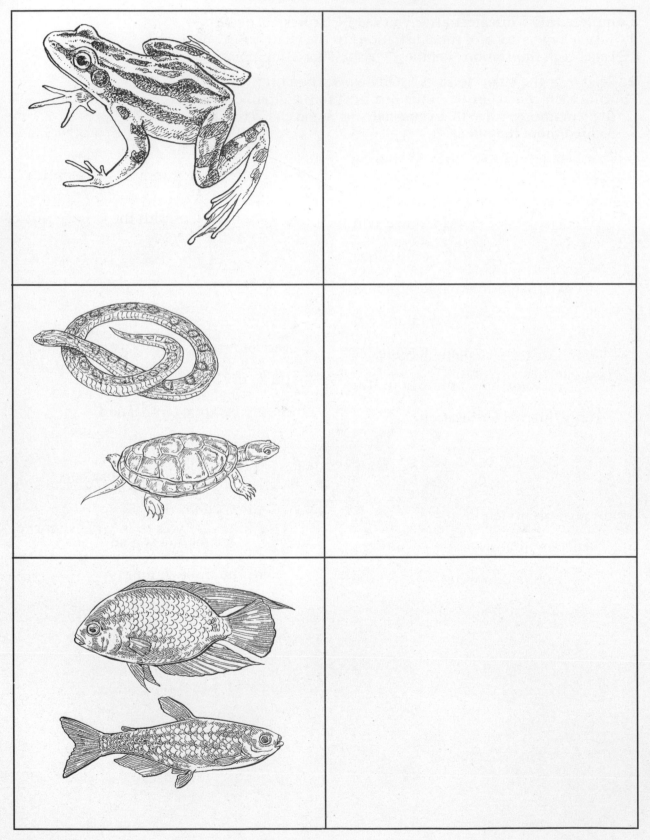

Copyright © by Holt, Rinehart and Winston. All rights reserved.

CHAPTER

16 VOCABULARY REVIEW WORKSHEET

Fishin' for Vertebrates

Complete this puzzle after you finish reading Chapter 16.

ACROSS

1. crocodiles, turtles, and snakes

6. system of tiny rows of sense organs along the sides of a fish's body

8. cartilaginous fishes store oil here to stay afloat

9. group of fishes with skeletons made of bone and swim bladders

10. aquatic larva of an amphibian

11. balloonlike organ that gives bony fish buoyancy

14. an animal that maintains a constant body temperature

16. bony structures covering the skin of bony fishes

21. body parts of a fish that remove oxygen from water and carbon dioxide from blood

22. prehistoric reptile ancestor of mammals

23. frogs use a vocal sac to do this

24. structures made of bone contained in the fins of perch, minnows, and eels

25. hard-shelled reptiles that live only on land

DOWN

2. fertilization of an egg that occurs inside the female's body

3. fertilization of an egg that occurs outside the female's body

4. the first fishes were this type of fish

5. an animal with a body temperature that fluctuates with the temperature of its environment

7. an egg that is usually surrounded by a hard shell

12. small, toothlike structures on the skin of cartilaginous fishes

13. a change from a larval form to an adult form

15. sharks and skates are this type of fish

17. saclike organs that take oxygen from the air and deliver it to the blood

18. an animal with a skull and a backbone

19. these fishes have air sacs and can gulp air

20. fanlike structures that help fish move, steer, stop, balance

Copyright © by Holt, Rinehart and Winston. All rights reserved.

Fishin' for Vertebrates, continued

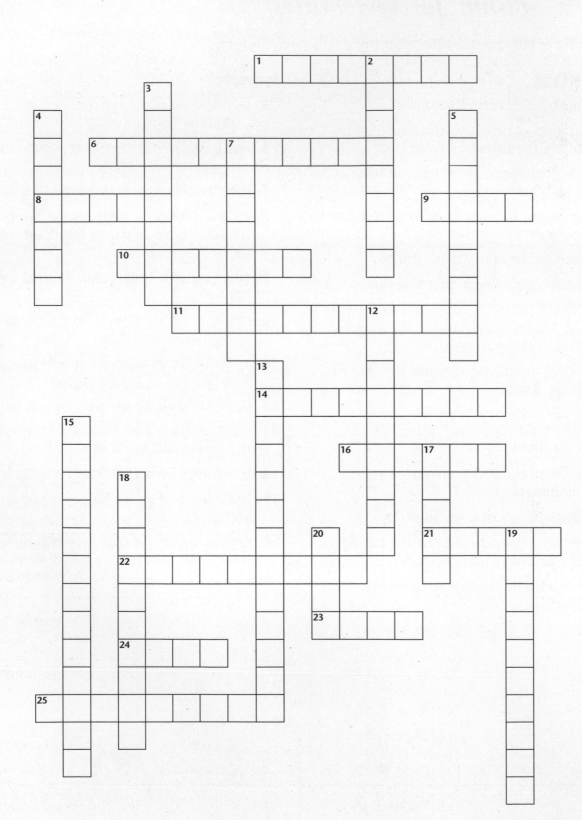

Copyright © by Holt, Rinehart and Winston. All rights reserved.

CHAPTER

17 REINFORCEMENT WORKSHEET

Mammals Are Us

Complete this worksheet after you finish reading Chapter 17, Section 2.

Each of the following terms is either an order of animals or an example of a particular order. Use the characteristics and facts in the table below to identify the order and one example of each group of animals, and record the corresponding terms in the spaces provided.

dolphin	cetaceans	hoofed mammals	sirenia
rabbit	human	carnivores	rodents
porcupine	aardvark	cow	toothless mammals
primates	manatee	Siberian tiger	
insectivores	lagomorphs	hedgehog	

Order	Characteristic	Example	An interesting fact
_____	generally eat insects and have long, sticky tongues	_____	only one is truly "toothless"
_____	tend to have pointed noses for digging	_____	live on all continents but Australia
_____	small animals that have sharp front teeth for gnawing	_____	front teeth never stop growing
_____	have strong legs for jumping, sensitive noses, and big ears	_____	some gather plants and shape them in "haystacks" to dry
_____	have eyes that face forward and opposable thumbs	_____	considered the most intelligent mammals
_____	eat mostly meat	_____	most have special teeth for slicing meat
_____	generally fast runners; they have flat teeth for chewing plants	_____	divided into groups according to the number of toes
_____	water-dwelling mammals that resemble fish	_____	use echolocation like bats do
_____	eat seaweed and water plants	_____	only four species in this order

Copyright © by Holt, Rinehart and Winston. All rights reserved.

CHAPTER

17 **VOCABULARY REVIEW WORKSHEET**

Is It a Bird or a Mammal?

Complete this worksheet after you finish reading Chapter 17.
Match each description in the second column with the correct term in the first column, and write the corresponding letter in the space provided.

_____ 1. primates

_____ 2. contour feathers

_____ 3. carnivores

_____ 4. down feathers

_____ 5. gestation period

_____ 6. preening

_____ 7. placenta

_____ 8. lift

_____ 9. placental mammals

_____ 10. brooding

_____ 11. marsupials

_____ 12. precocial chicks

_____ 13. monotremes

_____ 14. altricial chicks

_____ 15. therapsids

_____ 16. mammary glands

_____ 17. diaphragm

a. a large muscle at the bottom of the rib cage that helps bring air into the lungs

b. a mammal that nourishes its unborn offspring with a special organ inside the uterus

c. the time during which an embryo develops within the mother

d. a group of mammals that have opposable thumbs and binocular vision; includes humans, apes, and monkeys

e. chicks that hatch weak, naked, and helpless

f. a special organ of exchange that provides a developing fetus with nutrients and oxygen

g. mammals that lay eggs

h. prehistoric reptile ancestors of mammals

i. consumers that eat animals

j. feathers made of a stiff central shaft with many side branches called barbs

k. fluffy, insulating feathers that lie next to a bird's body

l. glands that secrete a nutritious fluid called milk

m. the upward pressure on the wing of a bird that keeps a bird in the air

n. when a bird uses its beak to spread oil on its feathers

o. chicks that hatch fully active

p. when a bird sits on its eggs until they hatch

q. a mammal that gives birth to partially developed, live young that develop inside the mother's pouch or skin fold

Copyright © by Holt, Rinehart and Winston. All rights reserved.

Name _____ Date _____ Class _____

Weaving a Food Web

Complete this worksheet after you finish reading Chapter 18, Section 2.

Imagine that you are an ecologist cataloging the interactions in a salt-marsh community. Look at the illustration of some of the organisms that live in a salt marsh, and draw arrows between them to indicate how energy flows between organisms in this ecosystem.

The Salt-Marsh Ecosystem

1. What producer(s) is shown above?

_____

_____

2. What carnivore(s) is shown above?

_____

_____

3. What omnivore(s) is shown above?

_____

_____

Copyright © by Holt, Rinehart and Winston. All rights reserved.

Symbiotic Relationships

Complete this worksheet after you finish reading Chapter 18, Section 3.

In the space provided, indicate whether each of the following symbiotic relationships is an example of *mutualism, commensalism,* or *parasitism*.

1. Clownfish live among the poisonous tentacles of a sea anemone. The clownfish are protected from predators, and they keep the sea anemone clean. _____

2. Barnacles attach themselves to the shells of crabs. The barnacles receive a home and transportation. _____

3. Bees use a flower's nectar for food, and they carry a flower's pollen to other flowers, allowing the flowers to reproduce. _____

4. Dutch elm disease has caused mass destruction of elms. The fungus feeds on materials produced by the elm trees. _____

5. Orchids grow in tree branches. The orchids receive light, and their roots get water from the air. _____

6. Small mites live on your skin, eating dead skin cells. _____

7. Lichens are composed of a fungus and an alga. The alga makes food through photosynthesis, and this food is used by the fungus and the alga. The fungus absorbs nutrients from the environment that are used by the fungus and the alga. _____

8. Tapeworms live in the intestines of cats, where they absorb nutrients from the food the cats eat. _____

Copyright © by Holt, Rinehart and Winston. All rights reserved.

Name _____ Date _____ Class _____

Environmental Enigma

Try this puzzle after you finish Chapter 18.

Using each of the clues below, fill in the letters of the word or phrase being described in the blanks provided on the next page.

1. a symbiotic relationship in which both organisms benefit

2. the study of the interactions between organisms and their environment

3. long-term change that takes place in two species because of their close interactions with each another

4. a group of individuals of the same species that live together in the same area at the same time

5. the environment where an organism lives

6. a consumer that eats animals

7. nonliving factors in the environment

8. symbiotic relationship in which one organism benefits and the other is not affected

9. an animal that feeds on the bodies of dead animals

10. two or more individuals or populations trying to use the same limited resource

11. diagram that represents how energy in food molecules flows from one organism to the next

12. consumer that eats a variety of organisms, both plants and animals

13. an organism that eats producers or other organisms for energy

14. triangle-shaped diagram that shows the loss of energy at each level of a food chain

15. the part of the Earth where life exists

16. living factors in the environment

17. an organism's way of life within an ecosystem

18. symbiotic relationship in which one organism benefits while the other is harmed

19. diagram that represents the many energy pathways in a real ecosystem

20. a consumer that eats plants

21. an organism that eats other organisms, called prey

22. an organism that gets energy by breaking down the remains of dead organisms

23. a community of organisms and their nonliving environment

Copyright © by Holt, Rinehart and Winston. All rights reserved.

Environmental Enigma, continued

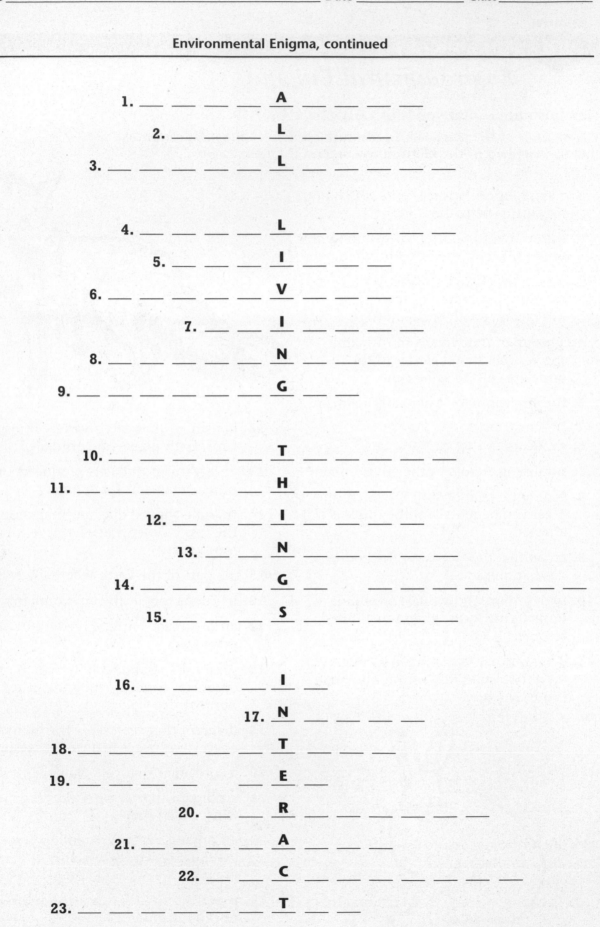

1. __ __ __ __ **A** __ __ __ __

2. __ __ __ **L** __ __ __ __

3. __ __ __ __ **L** __ __ __ __ __

4. __ __ __ __ **L** __ __ __ __

5. __ __ __ __ **I** __ __ __ __

6. __ __ __ __ __ **V** __

7. __ __ **I** __ __ __ __

8. __ __ __ __ __ **N** __ __ __ __

9. __ __ __ __ __ __ __ **G** __

10. __ __ __ __ __ **T** __ __ __ __

11. __ __ __ __ __ **H** __ __ __ __

12. __ __ __ __ __ **I** __ __ __ __

13. __ __ **N** __ __ __ __ __

14. __ __ __ **G** __ __ __ __ __ __ __ __

15. __ __ __ __ **S** __ __ __ __

16. __ __ __ __ __ **I** __ __

17. **N** __ __ __ __

18. __ __ __ __ __ **T** __ __ __

19. __ __ __ __ __ **E** __ __ __

20. __ __ __ **R** __ __ __ __ __

21. __ __ __ __ __ **A** __ __ __

22. __ __ __ **C** __ __ __ __ __

23. __ __ __ __ __ **T** __ __

Copyright © by Holt, Rinehart and Winston. All rights reserved.

What Goes Around . . .

Complete this worksheet after reading Chapter 19, Section 1.
Diagrams of the carbon cycle and water cycle are shown below and
on the next page. The opposing processes in both cycles are represented as arrows. Answer the questions relating to each diagram.

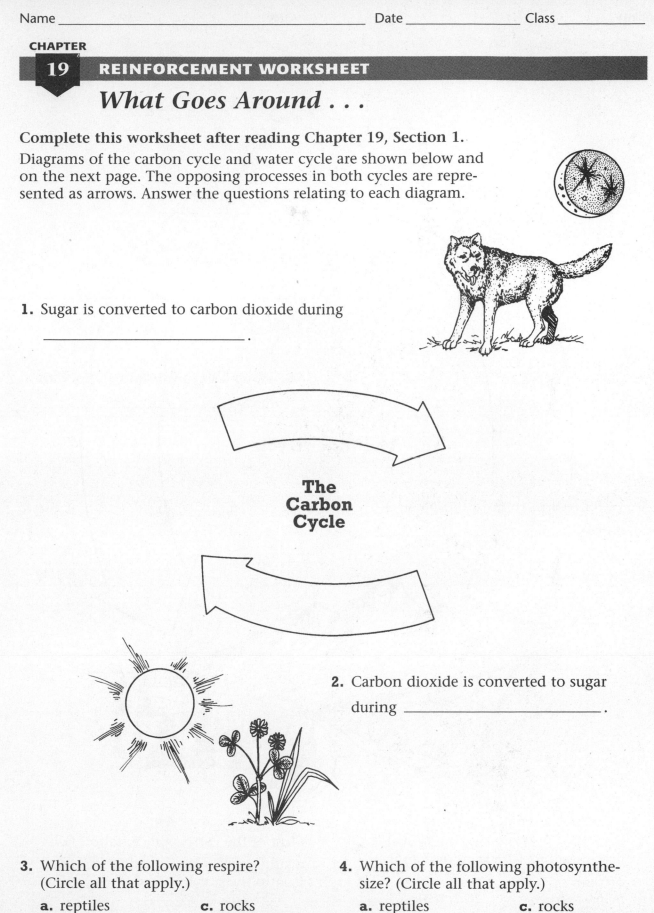

1. Sugar is converted to carbon dioxide during

_____ .

**The
Carbon
Cycle**

2. Carbon dioxide is converted to sugar

during _____ .

3. Which of the following respire?
(Circle all that apply.)

   a. reptiles   **c.** rocks
   b. plants   **d.** mammals

4. Which of the following photosynthesize? (Circle all that apply.)

   a. reptiles   **c.** rocks
   b. plants   **d.** mammals

Copyright © by Holt, Rinehart and Winston. All rights reserved.

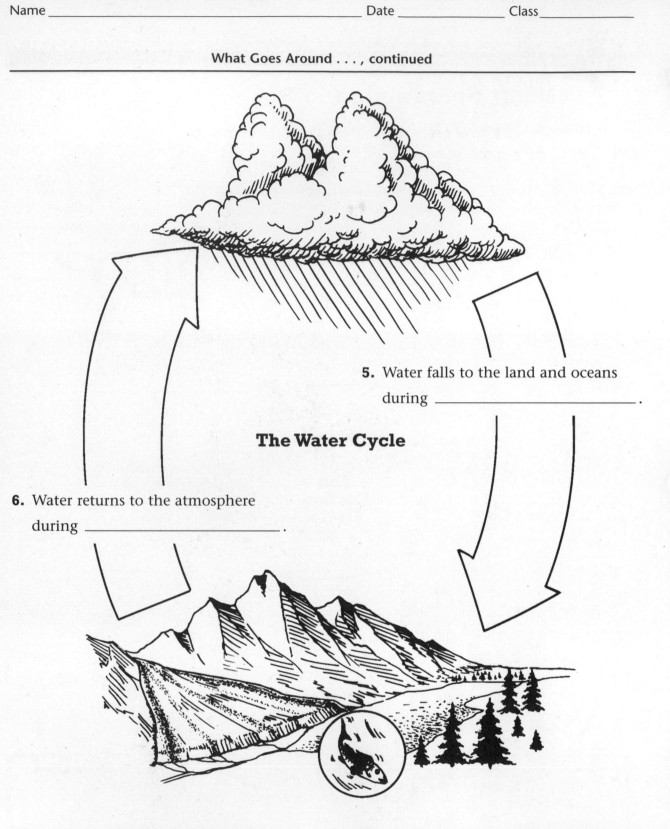

5. Water falls to the land and oceans during _____ .

The Water Cycle

6. Water returns to the atmosphere during _____ .

7. Which of the following are forms of precipitation? (Circle all that apply.)

   a. rain   **c.** snow

   b. meteorites   **d.** hail

8. Most of the Earth's precipitation falls

   a. into lakes.   **c.** onto land.

   b. into the oceans.   **d.** on organisms.

Copyright © by Holt, Rinehart and Winston. All rights reserved.

Name _____ Date _____ Class _____

CHAPTER

19 VOCABULARY REVIEW WORKSHEET

Cycle Search

After reading Chapter 19, give this puzzle a try!

The clues on this page will help you find the words in the puzzle on the next page. Write the answers next to the clues and circle the words in the puzzle.

1. water located within the rocks below the Earth's surface

2. anything that has volume and mass

3. the burning of fuel

4. the development of a community where no life had existed before

5. the process of changing atmospheric nitrogen into forms that plants can use

6. Sugar molecules are broken down to release energy.

7. the movement of carbon through the environment and living things

8. water, in solid or liquid form, that falls from the atmosphere to the Earth

9. the movement of water among the oceans, atmosphere, land, and living things

10. the ecological development of a community

11. the breakdown of dead materials

12. the movement of nitrogen through the environment and living organisms

13. the redevelopment of a community after an ecological disturbance

14. the first species to colonize a lifeless area

Copyright © by Holt, Rinehart and Winston. All rights reserved.

Cycle Search, continued

S	K	S	J	W	O	D	P	G	U	Y	H	C	A	E	Q	T	F	M	X	I
B	E	L	I	N	S	G	D	N	I	T	R	O	G	E	N	C	Y	C	L	E
H	I	C	J	K	W	R	U	V	W	O	Q	D	B	B	A	N	A	N	A	N
M	P	I	O	N	E	E	R	S	P	E	C	I	E	S	P	O	O	O	O	G
A	E	C	F	N	E	Y	N	I	E	T	O	R	P	L	N	I	R	I	S	T
G	R	O	U	N	D	W	A	T	E	R	V	I	C	H	S	T	T	T	K	B
X	Y	M	I	O	Q	A	J	D	R	E	V	W	I	S	R	A	M	I	F	G
T	A	B	B	L	T	S	R	E	M	A	T	T	E	R	T	R	H	S	S	X
R	C	U	K	T	S	A	E	Y	N	L	A	C	V	I	L	I	P	O	Y	I
O	B	S	A	T	I	N	M	E	S	O	C	U	P	Q	I	P	U	P	P	Y
W	A	T	E	R	C	Y	C	L	E	U	H	I	D	O	J	S	A	M	E	X
F	G	I	R	U	K	H	R	O	S	I	C	K	B	E	D	E	S	O	T	O
M	M	O	A	B	G	I	R	Y	L	E	Y	C	P	S	I	R	H	C	V	X
C	S	N	T	U	K	F	R	I	R	B	E	Y	E	B	S	I	A	E	X	S
G	R	O	U	P	Q	A	D	P	S	H	Y	N	O	S	A	L	A	D	J	L
M	B	I	O	T	M	U	S	T	S	U	C	C	E	S	S	I	O	N	V	W
X	F	E	N	I	T	R	O	G	E	N	F	I	X	A	T	I	O	N	N	O
C	C	A	R	B	O	N	C	Y	C	L	E	A	U	Q	E	H	O	D	T	P
J	K	P	L	I	P	Y	K	I	W	D	G	N	U	P	R	H	I	N	E	J

Copyright © by Holt, Rinehart and Winston. All rights reserved.

CHAPTER
20 **REINFORCEMENT WORKSHEET**

Know Your Biomes

Complete this worksheet after you have finished reading Chapter 20, Section 1.

1. Using the Temperature & rainfall column as a guide, label the biomes using the following terms: *desert, tropical rain forest, arctic tundra, coniferous forest, temperate grassland, savanna,* and *temperate deciduous forest.*

2. Use the examples and characteristics given in the box on the next page to fill in the appropriate blanks.

Type of biome	Temperature & rainfall	Examples & characteristics
_____	summer: 38°C winter: 7°C rain: less than 25 cm per year	jack rabbit _____ _____
_____	dry season: 34°C wet season: 16°C rain: 150 cm per year	has scattered clumps of trees _____ _____
_____	daytime: 34°C nighttime: 20°C rain: up to 400 cm per year	the most biologically diverse biome _____ _____
_____	summer: 28°C winter: 6°C rain: 75–125 cm per year	woody shrubs beneath tree layer _____ _____

Copyright © by Holt, Rinehart and Winston. All rights reserved.

Type of biome	Temperature & rainfall	Examples & characteristics
_____	summer: 12°C winter: −26°C rain: 30–50 cm per year	has no trees _____ _____
_____	summer: 14°C winter: −10°C rain: 35–75 cm per year	waxy coating on needles _____ _____
_____	summer: 30°C winter: 0°C rain: 25–75 cm per year	has few slow-growing plants _____ _____

EXAMPLES AND CHARACTERISTICS

musk ox
bison
giraffe
woodpecker
porcupine
animals prefer life in the treetops
most animals are active at night
trees produce seeds in cones
very few trees
plants spaced far apart
permafrost
trees lose leaves in fall
diverse groups of herbivores live here
most nutrients in the vegetation

Copyright © by Holt, Rinehart and Winston. All rights reserved.

Eco-Puzzle

After you finish Chapter 20, give this puzzle a try!

In the space provided, write the term described by the clue. Then find those words in the puzzle. Terms can be hidden in the puzzle vertically, horizontally, diagonally, or backward.

1. a biome in the far north where no trees can grow

_____

2. a tree that produces seeds in a cone _____

3. soil that is always frozen _____

4. a hot, dry biome that receives less than 25 cm of rain a year

_____

5. the zone of a lake or pond closest to the edge of the land

_____

6. a treeless wetland ecosystem _____

7. microscopic photosynthetic organisms in the ocean

_____

8. geographic area characterized by certain types of plants and

animals _____

9. trees that lose their leaves in the fall

_____

10. a wetland ecosystem with trees _____

11. an algae that forms rafts in the Sargasso Sea

_____

12. an area where fresh and salty waters constantly mix

_____

13. land where the water level is near or above the surface of the

ground for most of the year _____

14. very small consumers in the ocean _____

15. a tropical grassland with scattered clumps of trees

_____

16. a small stream or river that flows into a larger one

_____

17. nonliving factors in the environment

_____

Copyright © by Holt, Rinehart and Winston. All rights reserved.

Name_____ Date _____ Class_____

Eco-Puzzle, continued

18. a measure of the number of species an area contains

_____

T	S	O	N	O	D	E	S	E	R	T	A	R	I	N	Z	X
U	V	C	W	T	R	I	B	U	E	Z	P	C	H	O	V	G
N	B	Q	E	F	E	G	C	L	L	I	T	T	O	R	A	L
D	L	S	T	S	O	R	F	A	M	R	E	P	Q	U	L	B
R	H	A	L	P	E	M	A	F	P	O	L	N	B	K	S	C
A	O	V	A	R	C	X	S	A	R	A	O	J	T	W	G	F
P	Y	D	N	D	V	F	J	C	N	T	G	O	A	Y	E	D
H	R	I	D	E	A	R	W	K	K	Y	N	M	C	M	H	S
Y	A	V	R	C	L	S	T	N	B	L	P	Z	O	X	L	A
T	U	E	M	I	Q	O	A	G	Q	C	I	I	N	K	Z	N
O	T	R	Y	D	N	L	P	R	M	O	B	T	I	R	O	N
P	S	S	C	U	P	I	B	E	G	K	F	V	F	Q	O	A
Z	E	I	Q	O	M	W	E	T	L	A	T	B	E	J	P	V
A	G	T	T	U	N	D	L	F	D	O	S	G	R	L	L	A
I	W	Y	R	S	C	I	T	O	I	B	A	S	O	N	B	S
V	H	E	A	B	M	A	R	S	H	N	D	L	U	W	T	E
P	D	J	L	C	Y	R	A	T	U	B	I	R	T	M	N	V

Copyright © by Holt, Rinehart and Winston. All rights reserved.

CHAPTER
21 **REINFORCEMENT WORKSHEET**

It's "R" Planet!

Complete this worksheet after you finish reading Chapter 21, Section 2.

Use terms, definitions, and conservation suggestions from the lists below to design a flier that will encourage students in your school to participate in conservation. Get students' attention by making your flier colorful, using a catch phrase, or by using any other method you can think of. Your job is to make other students aware of the role they can play in protecting our environment. There's a sample flier on the next page.

- the three R's: reduce, reuse, recycle
- conservation: preserving resources
- recycling: breaking down trash in order to use it again
- resource recovery: turning garbage into electricity

- maintain biodiversity
- protect endangered species
- protect habitats
- enforce the Endangered Species Act

- to reduce means to use less
- to reuse means to use it again
- to recycle is a type of reuse

- plastics
- paper products
- waste wood
- glass
- cardboard
- cans

- use cloth napkins
- walk, ride a bike, or use public transportation
- use rechargeable batteries
- turn off lights, lamps, and computers when not in use

Copyright © by Holt, Rinehart and Winston. All rights reserved.

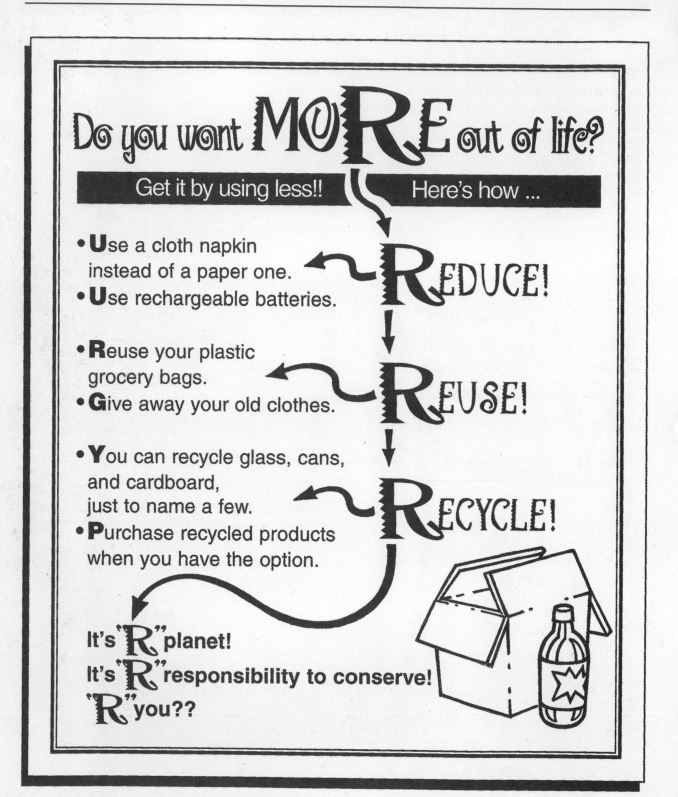

Do you want **MORE** out of life?

Get it by using less!!   **Here's how ...**

REDUCE!

- **U**se a cloth napkin instead of a paper one.
- **U**se rechargeable batteries.

REUSE!

- **R**euse your plastic grocery bags.
- **G**ive away your old clothes.

RECYCLE!

- **Y**ou can recycle glass, cans, and cardboard, just to name a few.
- **P**urchase recycled products when you have the option.

It's "R" planet!
It's "R" responsibility to conserve!
"R" you??

Copyright © by Holt, Rinehart and Winston. All rights reserved.

Solve the Environmental Puzzle

Give this puzzle a try after you finish Chapter 21.

Using each of the clues below, fill in the letters of the term described in the blanks provided on the next page.

1. can be broken down by the environment

2. process of transforming garbage into electricity

3. type of hazardous wastes that take hundreds or thousands of years to become harmless

4. when the number of individuals becomes so large that they can't get all the resources they need

5. the process of making new products from reprocessed used products

6. the clearing of forest lands

7. the world around us

8. an organism that makes a home for itself in a new place

9. harmful substances in the environment

10. a girl who developed a way to make paper without cutting down a tree

11. describes a natural resource that can be used and replaced over a relatively short time

12. describes a natural resource that cannot be replaced or can be replaced only after thousands or millions of years

13. substances used to kill crop-destroying insects

14. the preservation of resources

15. the number and variety of living things

16. poisonous

17. the presence of harmful substances in the environment

18. protective layer of the atmosphere destroyed by CFCs

Copyright © by Holt, Rinehart and Winston. All rights reserved.

Solve the Environmental Puzzle, continued

1. __ __ __ __ __ __ **R** __ __ __ __ __ __ __

2. __ __ __ __ __ __ __ __ __ **E** __ __ __ __ __

3. __ __ **D** __ __ __ __ __ __ __ __

4. __ __ __ __ __ __ __ **U** __ __ __ __ __ __

5. __ __ **C** __ __ __ __ __ __ __

6. __ __ __ __ __ __ **E** __ __ __ __ __ __

7. __ __ __ __ **R** __ __ __ __ __ __

8. __ __ __ __ **E** __

9. __ __ __ __ __ **U** __ __ __ __

10. __ __ __ __ __   __ __ __ __ __ __ **S** __

11. __ __ __ **E** __ __ __ __ __

12. __ __ **R** __ __ __ __ __ __ __ __

13. __ **E** __ __ __ __ __ __ __ __ __ __

14. **C** __ __ __ __ __ __ __ __ __ __ __ __ __

15. __ __ __ __ __ __ __ __ **Y**

16. __ __ __ **C**

17. __ __ **L** __ __ __ __

18. __ __ __ __ **E**

Copyright © by Holt, Rinehart and Winston. All rights reserved.

CHAPTER
22 **REINFORCEMENT WORKSHEET**

The Hipbone's Connected to the . . .

Complete this worksheet after you finish reading Chapter 22, Section 2.

Your skeleton makes it possible for you to move. It provides your organs with protection, stores minerals, makes white and red blood cells, and supports your body. Look at the human skeleton below, and write the names of the major bones listed below in the spaces provided.

Bones

- humerus
- fibula
- pelvic girdle
- radius
- patella
- ulna
- ribs
- skull
- clavicle
- vertebral column
- femur
- tibia

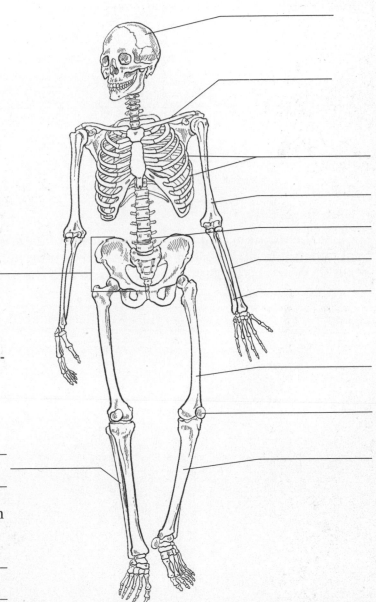

The place where two or more bones connect is called a joint. In the chapter, you looked at fixed, ball-and-socket, and hinge joints.

1. What kind of joint is the elbow?

_____

_____

2. What kind of joint allows the arm to move freely in all directions?

_____

_____

_____

Copyright © by Holt, Rinehart and Winston. All rights reserved.

CHAPTER

22 **REINFORCEMENT WORKSHEET**

Muscle Map

Complete this worksheet after you finish reading Chapter 22, Section 3.

Each of the boxes below represents one of the three types of muscle tissue in your body. Write the notes in the appropriate box. Some of the notes can be used more than once.

Three Types of Muscle

Skeletal	Cardiac	Smooth

Notes

- moves bones
- involuntary
- voluntary
- often works in pairs
- in the heart
- in blood vessels
- in the digestive tract

Look at the diagram of a human leg below. A flexor is a muscle that bends a part of your body when it contracts, and an extensor is a muscle that extends a part of your body when it contracts. Label the flexor muscle and the extensor muscle on the diagram below.

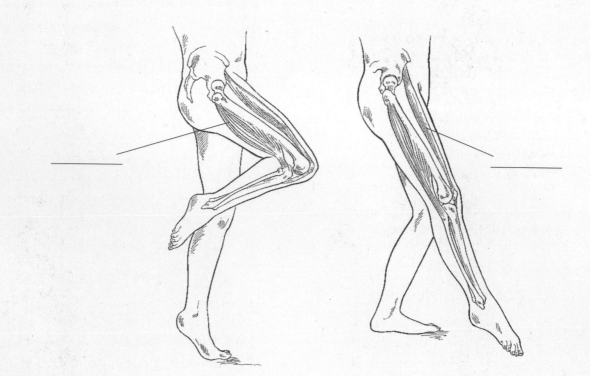

Copyright © by Holt, Rinehart and Winston. All rights reserved.

CHAPTER 22

VOCABULARY REVIEW WORKSHEET

A Connective Crossword

Give this crossword puzzle a try after you finish reading Chapter 22!
Solve the clues below, and write the answers in the appropriate
spaces in the crossword puzzle.

ACROSS

3. _____ is the type of bone tissue that gives a bone its strength. (two words)

8. place where two or more bones connect

10. small organs that produce a salty liquid that flows to the surface of the skin (two words)

11. _____ is the type of bone tissue that contains marrow. (two words)

17. Your _____ is made up of your skin, hair, and nails. (two words)

21. strong elastic bands of connective tissue that keep joints together

22. small organs in the dermis that produce hair (two words)

23. a group of similar cells working together

24. _____ is the type of tissue made of cells that contract and relax to produce movement. (two words)

25. _____ tissue sends electrical signals through the body.

DOWN

1. two or more tissues working together

2. soft, flexible tissue that is found in the tip of your nose

3. _____ is the type of tissue that joins, supports, protects, insulates, and cushions organs. (two words)

4. the thin, outermost layer of skin

5. a muscle that straightens a body part

6. maintenance of a stable internal environment

7. strands of tough connective tissue that connect skeletal muscles to bones

9. _____ is found in the digestive tract and blood vessels. (two words)

12. _____ is the type of tissue that covers and protects underlying tissue. (two words)

13. a muscle that bends a body part

14. _____ muscle is found only in the heart.

15. thick layer of skin found under item 4 down

16. a collection of organs whose primary function is movement (two words)

18. _____ are muscles that move bones. (two words)

19. made up of bones, cartilage, and the special structures that connect them (two words)

20. a darkening chemical in skin that determines skin color

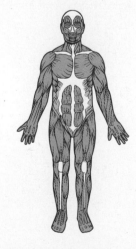

Copyright © by Holt, Rinehart and Winston. All rights reserved.

A Connective Crossword, continued

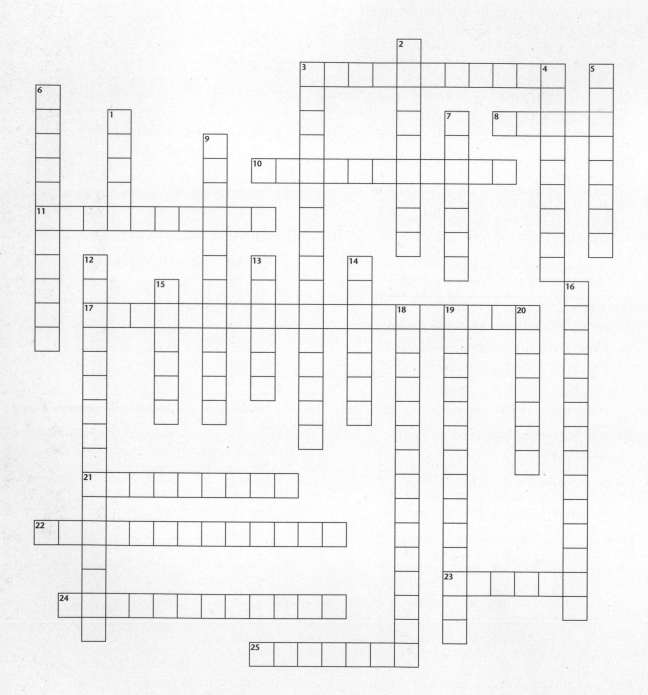

Copyright © by Holt, Rinehart and Winston. All rights reserved.

Name _____ Date _____ Class _____

Matchmaker, Matchmaker

Complete this worksheet after you finish reading Chapter 23, Section 1.

As you learned in this chapter, different blood types have different antigens and antibodies. Antigens are chemicals on the surface of red blood cells. Antibodies are chemicals in the blood's plasma. A person makes antibodies against the antigens that their red blood cells do not have. Those antibodies will attack any red blood cell that has those antigens, causing the red blood cells to clump together.

Antigens and Antibodies Present in Blood Types

Blood type	Antigens	Antibodies
O	none	A, B
A	A	B
B	B	A
AB	A, B	none

A person can receive blood from another person if the donor's blood does not contain antigens that the antibodies of the receiver's blood will attack. Complete the table below by writing *yes* or *no* in each of the blanks.

Receiver's blood type	Can receive type O?	Can receive type A?	Can receive type B?	Can receive type AB?
O				
A				
B				
AB				

1. Which blood type do you think a hospital would find the most useful? Explain.

_____

_____

_____

_____

Copyright © by Holt, Rinehart and Winston. All rights reserved.

Colors of the Heart

Complete this worksheet after you finish reading Chapter 23, Section 1.
You will need red and blue colored pencils or crayons for this worksheet.

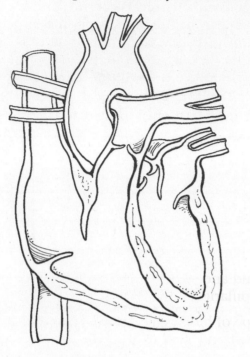

> **HELPFUL HINT**
>
> The left ventricle and atrium of this heart are on the right side of the page.

1. The atria are the upper chambers of the heart. The ventricles are the lower chambers of the heart. Label the atria and the ventricles on the diagram.

2. Oxygen-rich blood flows through a vein from the lungs into the left atrium. Color the left atrium and the vein that carries the blood from the lungs red.

3. Blood flows from the left atrium to the left ventricle. Color the left ventricle red.

4. Blood flows through an artery from the left ventricle to the body. The body takes up the oxygen in the blood. Color this artery red.

5. Blood flows through two large veins from the body into the right atrium. Color the right atrium and the two large veins blue.

6. Blood flows from the right atrium to the right ventricle. Color the right ventricle blue.

7. Blood flows through an artery from the right ventricle to the lungs. In the lungs, the blood picks up oxygen. Color this artery blue.

8. Add arrows to your diagram to indicate the flow of blood through the heart. Indicate whether each blood vessel is carrying blood to or from the lungs or the body.

Copyright © by Holt, Rinehart and Winston. All rights reserved.

CHAPTER
23 **VOCABULARY REVIEW WORKSHEET**

A Hunt with Heart

After finishing Chapter 23, give this puzzle a try!

Solve the clues below. Then use the clues to complete the puzzle on the next page.

1. _____ system that transports materials to and from the body's cells

2. _____ a connective tissue made up of cells, cell parts, and plasma

3. _____ the fluid part of blood

4. _____ largest lymph organ

5. _____ upper portion of the throat

6. _____ system that collects extracellular fluid and returns it to your blood

7. _____ lymph organ just above the heart that produces lymphocytes

8. _____ fluid and particles absorbed into lymph capillaries

9. _____ type of blood circulation between the heart and the lungs

10. _____ the smallest blood vessels in the body

11. _____ your voice box

12. _____ expressed in millimeters of Mercury (mm Hg)

13. _____ cell fragments that clump together to form a plug that helps reduce blood loss

14. _____ small bean-shaped organs that remove particles from lymph

15. _____ process that is made up of breathing and cellular respiration

16. _____ type of blood circulation between the heart and the rest of the body

17. _____ dome-shaped muscle involved in breathing

18. _____ upper heart chambers

19. _____ blood vessels that direct blood away from the heart

20. _____ made up of groups of lymphatic tissue located inside your throat, at the back of your nasal cavity, and at the back of your tongue

Copyright © by Holt, Rinehart and Winston. All rights reserved.

A Hunt with Heart, continued

21. _____ this system consists of the lungs, the throat, and the passageways that lead to the lungs

22. _____ lower heart chambers

23. _____ blood vessels that direct blood toward the heart

24. _____ tiny sacs that form the bronchiole branches of the lungs

25. _____ your windpipe

26. _____ the two tubes that connect the lungs with the trachea

How many chapter concepts can you find in the block of letters below? Use the clues to help you find them. Words may appear horizontally, vertically, diagonally, or backward.

G	L	Y	M	P	H	A	T	I	C	I	M	E	T	S	Y	S	A
T	I	A	L	V	E	O	L	I	T	O	L	N	M	O	V	L	O
O	B	S	U	R	D	S	H	U	O	C	T	E	F	O	S	Y	S
N	E	L	A	O	E	C	P	A	B	C	A	C	L	Q	Y	M	C
S	H	T	O	I	N	T	H	Y	T	A	P	L	I	M	R	P	A
I	I	L	R	O	X	Y	L	N	D	R	X	N	Y	R	A	H	P
L	B	A	R	O	D	D	T	B	I	D	I	T	R	E	N	N	I
S	Y	B	L	B	I	P	C	Y	G	I	S	A	O	S	O	O	L
E	B	M	A	R	A	L	R	S	U	O	B	O	T	P	M	D	L
L	M	L	P	R	P	A	H	E	E	V	I	X	A	I	L	E	A
C	A	H	G	H	H	T	U	I	S	A	R	L	R	R	U	S	R
I	W	R	O	R	R	E	S	R	P	S	D	T	I	A	P	U	I
R	X	N	Y	R	A	L	E	E	L	C	U	B	P	T	J	M	E
T	C	T	V	S	G	E	Y	T	E	U	P	R	S	I	E	U	S
N	C	A	N	D	M	T	K	R	E	L	I	E	E	O	S	S	R
E	P	E	P	L	A	S	M	A	N	A	Y	M	R	N	T	E	I
V	E	I	N	S	U	M	Y	H	T	R	A	C	H	E	A	Z	N

Copyright © by Holt, Rinehart and Winston. All rights reserved.

CHAPTER
24 **REINFORCEMENT WORKSHEET**

Annie Apple's Amazing Adventure

Complete this worksheet after you finish reading Chapter 24, Section 2.

Being an apple, Annie is just not very good with words. In her story below she used many terms incorrectly. The incorrect terms have been underlined and numbered. Help Annie by writing the correct term in the corresponding blank provided at the bottom of the page.

Hi, my name is Annie Apple, and I'm, well, an apple! I've just been on the strangest adventure, and I thought you'd like to hear about it.

First, this girl took a huge bite out of me and used her teeth to chew me. They call that (1) chemical digestion. While this was happening I got soaked by (2) bile, which breaks down my carbohydrates into simple sugars. Boy, was that uncomfortable! Then I was swallowed.

I went down a long tube called the (3) small intestine, and I ended up in the (4) liver. There, I was bombarded by acid and enzymes, which broke me down further until I was a soupy mixture called (5) anus. Next I was released into the (6) large intestine. There I was met by pancreatic juice and (7) saliva. Then I was broken down enough to be partially absorbed into the bloodstream.

After that, I passed into the (8) esophagus, where I had water absorbed from me. At last, what was left of me passed through an opening called the (9) villi. But that's not the end! The part of me that passed into the bloodstream provided energy to lots of cells before it ended up at the (10) stomach, where it was filtered through tiny (11) bladders and then went out the (12) urethra to be stored in the (13) nephron.

The final leg of my journey was through the (14) ureter to the outside world. Isn't that an unbelievable adventure?

---

1. _____
2. _____
3. _____
4. _____
5. _____
6. _____
7. _____

8. _____
9. _____
10. _____
11. _____
12. _____
13. _____
14. _____

Copyright © by Holt, Rinehart and Winston. All rights reserved.

CHAPTER
24 **VOCABULARY REVIEW WORKSHEET**

Alien Anagrams

After you finish reading Chapter 24, give this puzzle a try!

A spaceship full of alien ambassadors has just landed in your backyard. They are very interested in earthling science, especially the study of biological systems. Help them translate their scrambled list of terms. DOOG CLUK!

1. long, straight tube connecting your throat and stomach

GAPHOUSES _____

2. microscopic filters located in the kidneys

HORNPENS _____

3. large, reddish brown organ that helps with digestion

VLIRE _____

4. green liquid used in fat digestion

LEIB _____

5. rhythmic muscle contractions in the esophagus

STRASPELISI _____

6. digestion that involves breaking, crushing, and mashing of food

HELNAMACCI _____

7. tube that allows urine to leave the body

HURTEAR _____

8. last section of the large intestine

METRUC _____

9. muscular organ that squeezes food into chyme

THOSCAM _____

10. digestion that involves breaking down large molecules of food into nutrients

CLAMHICE _____

11. small, fingerlike projections of the wall of the small intestine

LIVLI _____

12. organ of the digestive and endocrine systems

SNARPACE _____

13. bean-shaped organs that filter blood

SKYNIED _____

14. baglike organ that stores bile

BALDGLARDLE _____

15. process of removing waste from the body

RICENOXET _____

16. where most chemical digestion occurs

SLALM SEENITINT _____

Copyright © by Holt, Rinehart and Winston. All rights reserved.

Name _____ Date _____ Class _____

This System Is Just "Two" Nervous!

Complete this worksheet after you finish reading Chapter 25, Section 1.

Did you know that all the different parts of your body are in constant conversation with one another? Well they are, even though you never hear a word of it! Most of your activities require your **nervous system** to respond to your environment. Read this imaginary conversation between the various parts of your nervous system, and then answer the questions that follow by using the boldface terms as answers.

Brain: Okay everybody, this is Mission Control for the **central** nervous system. It is time to get this body out of bed! Left Arm, would you please shut off the alarm clock already! With that racket, the **Cerebrum** is having trouble remembering what is on the exam in math class today. Left Arm, I am sending signals through **motor neurons** to your muscles now, and I expect you to obey those orders, pronto. Feet, it is time to hit the floor. Signals through your motor neurons are on the way too. This **voluntary movement** will get us to the closet so we can get dressed!

Stomach: Excuse me, but our blood sugar is getting low. It is awfully empty down here! We also realize that the skin **receptors** are detecting that the room is cold. The sooner we get dressed, the sooner we eat, so hurry!

Brain: I am sorry Stomach, but you will just have to wait. The arms are still involved with other voluntary movement—they are currently combing the hair. By the way, Heart, thank you for pumping all night. You kept us all alive and well. I really have to hand it to the organs on the **involuntary movement** team. This includes you too, Stomach—that late night snack before bed was great, and your digestion process went so smoothly!

Cerebrum: Aha, I've got it! We are having a quiz in math class today, not an exam. Whew, I am so glad I remembered! **Medulla**, I am sorry I didn't remember we needed a coat today. I felt the increase in heart rate you made as we ran back up the stairs. Even though you are only 3 cm long, we couldn't live without you, Medulla.

Spinal Cord: Good morning everyone! All my vertebrae are feeling great today. That new mattress is wonderful. Well, good grief, I have so many impulses from the neurons in the **peripheral** nervous system. The **dendrites** and **axons** of each neuron move information to and from other neurons so quickly. It is amazing I can keep up with you guys!

Peripheral Nervous System: Yes, well, thank you **Spinal Cord**. I have **nerves** throughout the body that I am responsible for, and there is never a moment to waste. I must transfer information to the central nervous system.

Copyright © by Holt, Rinehart and Winston. All rights reserved.

_____

This System Is Just "Two" Nervous! continued

_____

Left Hand: Ouch! Pain! Pain! Pain! Spinal Cord, help!

Spinal Cord: Left Hand, stop touching that hot mug!

Cerebellum: Watch out, Legs! Leg Muscles, this is the **Cerebellum**, be quick about it and step to the side, not to the back! You are about to trip over the dog!

Cerebrum: Hey, what just happened? I missed it.

Spinal Cord: Don't worry, Cerebrum, it was just another involuntary movement. The mug we grabbed was too hot to handle, so a reflex prevented the hands from getting burned. I took care of it since you are just too slow, but hey, that's my job.

Questions

1. The nervous system is made up of the _____ nervous system and the _____ nervous system.

2. The central nervous system is made up of the brain and the

   _____ .

3. The peripheral nervous system has many _____ throughout the body.

4. Combing your hair, getting out of bed, and getting dressed are all examples of _____ .

5. The process of digestion and the pumping your heart does are both examples of _____ .

6. The neurons in your body use _____ and _____ to transfer information.

7. The _____ is responsible for thinking and memory.

8. The _____ controls your heart rate, blood pressure, and involuntary breathing.

9. The _____ keeps track of the body's position.

10. _____ tell your muscles to move.

11. Sensory neurons use _____ to tell you when you are hungry and cold.

Copyright © by Holt, Rinehart and Winston. All rights reserved.

CHAPTER
25 **REINFORCEMENT WORKSHEET**

The Eyes Have It

Complete this worksheet after you finish reading Chapter 25, Section 2.

Match the descriptions in Column B with the correct structure in
Column A, and write the corresponding letter in the appropriate
space. When you have finished, use the words in Column A to label
the diagram.

Column A	Column B
____ **1.** rods	**a.** holds the photoreceptors
____ **2.** lens	**b.** give a view of the world in grays
____ **3.** optic nerve	**c.** changes pupil size to control the amount of light entering
____ **4.** cones	**d.** focuses light onto the retina
____ **5.** iris	**e.** allows light into the eye
____ **6.** pupil	**f.** interpret bright light; give a colorful view of the world
____ **7.** retina	**g.** takes impulses from the retina to the brain

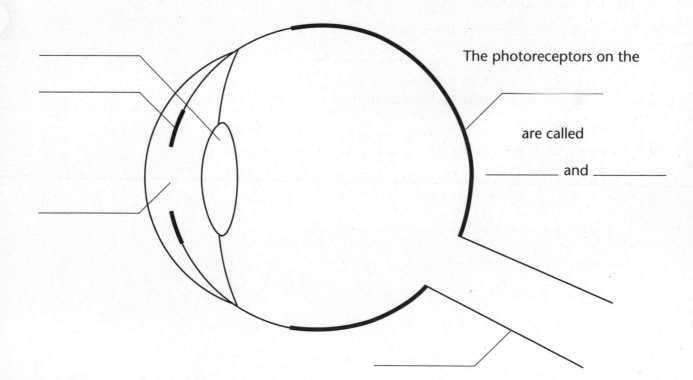

The photoreceptors on the

are called

_____ and _____

Copyright © by Holt, Rinehart and Winston. All rights reserved.

CHAPTER
25 **REINFORCEMENT WORKSHEET**

Every Gland Lends a Hand

Complete this worksheet after you finish reading Chapter 25, Section 3.

1. How many endocrine glands are discussed in this chapter?

_____

2. The _____ glands regulate the level of calcium in your blood.

3. Which gland controls blood-sugar levels?

_____

4. When your body responds to stress or danger, it uses the

_____ glands.

5. Which one of the glands helps your body fight disease?

_____

6. Your body uses chemical messengers released into the blood,

called _____ , to control body functions.

7. The _____ gland increases the rate at which you use energy.

8. Which glands are involved in reproduction?

_____ or _____

9. This gland has many functions, one of which is to help the thyroid function properly. Which gland is this?

_____

10. All these glands are part of the _____ system.

11. What are the functions of the endocrine system?

_____

_____

_____

_____

Copyright © by Holt, Rinehart and Winston. All rights reserved.

CHAPTER
25 **VOCABULARY REVIEW WORKSHEET**

Your Body's Own Language

Give this anagram a try after you finish reading Chapter 25!

1. system in your body responsible for gathering and interpreting information about the body's internal and external environment: URSVNEO

__ __ __ __ __ __ __

2. small snail-shaped organ of the inner ear: CHACOLE

__ __ __ __ __ __ __

3. subdivision of question 1; includes your brain and spinal cord: ANRCELT

__ __ __ __ __ __ __

4. subdivision of your nervous system; collection of nerves: LIPPERHARE

__ __ __ __ __ __ __ __ __ __

5. piece of curved material in the eye that focuses light on the retina: SLEN

__ __ __ __

6. specialized cells that transfer messages as electrical energy: NENORUS

__ __ __ __ __ __ __

7. special neurons in your eye that help you see color: SNOCE

__ __ __ __ __

8. short branched extensions through which question 6 receives signals: SERENDDIT

__ __ __ __ __ __ __ __ __

9. long cell fiber that transmits information to other cells: NOXA

__ __ __ __

10. type of neuron that gathers information about what is happening in and around your body: NYSSREO

__ __ __ __ __ __ __

11. group of cells that makes special chemicals for your body: GNALD

__ __ __ __ __

12. colored part of the eye: ISRI

__ __ __ __

13. specialized dendrites that detect changes inside or outside the body: OPETCRSER

__ __ __ __ __ __ __ __ __

Copyright © by Holt, Rinehart and Winston. All rights reserved.

14. send messages from the brain and spinal cord to other systems:
OMOTR EOSURNN

— — — — — —   — — — — — — —

15. axons that are bundled together with blood vessels and connective tissue: NSREVE

— — — — — —

16. the largest organ of the central nervous system: ARNIB

— — — — —

17. chemical messengers produced by the endocrine glands: SHORNMOE

— — — — — — — —

18. part of question 16 where thinking takes place: CREUMBER

— — — — — — — —

19. part of question 16 that helps you keep your balance: MULERBECLE

— — — — — — — — — —

20. transfers electrical impulses from the eye to the brain: COPTI VERNE

— — — — —   — — — — —

21. part of question 16 that connects to the spinal cord: DELUALM

— — — — — — —

22. a quick, involuntary action: FELEXR

— — — — — —

23. system that controls body functions such as sexual development: CODENINER

— — — — — — — — —

24. the light-sensitive layer of cells at the back of the eye: ETNRAI

— — — — — —

25. special neurons in the eye that detect light: EPSERROOPTHTCO

— — — — — — — — — — — — — —

26. electrical messages that pass along the neurons: SPULIMES

— — — — — — — —

27. type of question 25 that can detect very dim light: DSRO

— — — —

Copyright © by Holt, Rinehart and Winston. All rights reserved.

CHAPTER

26 REINFORCEMENT WORKSHEET

Reproduction Review

Complete this worksheet after you finish reading Chapter 26, Section 1.

Different organisms reproduce in different ways. Fill in the table below by circling the correct type of reproduction. Then indicate the organism's method of fertilization and where the embryo develops. Several boxes have been filled in to get you started.

Organism	Type of reproduction	Method of fertilization	Where the embryo develops
Hydra	asexual or sexual		none (no embryo)
Whale	asexual or sexual		
Chicken	asexual or sexual		
Frog	asexual or sexual		
Sea star	asexual or sexual	none	
Echidna	asexual or sexual		
Fish	asexual or sexual		
Human	asexual or sexual		inside the mother (placental)
Kangaroo	asexual or sexual		

Copyright © by Holt, Rinehart and Winston. All rights reserved.

Name _____ Date _____ Class _____

The Beginning of a Life

Complete this worksheet after you have finished reading Chapter 26, Section 3.

The following illustration shows the development of a human. Choose the term from the list below left that best labels what is indicated in the diagram, and write the term in the corresponding box. Then, match each feature below right to the stage where it develops, and write the corresponding letter in the blank. Each feature and term is used once. Stages may have more than one feature.

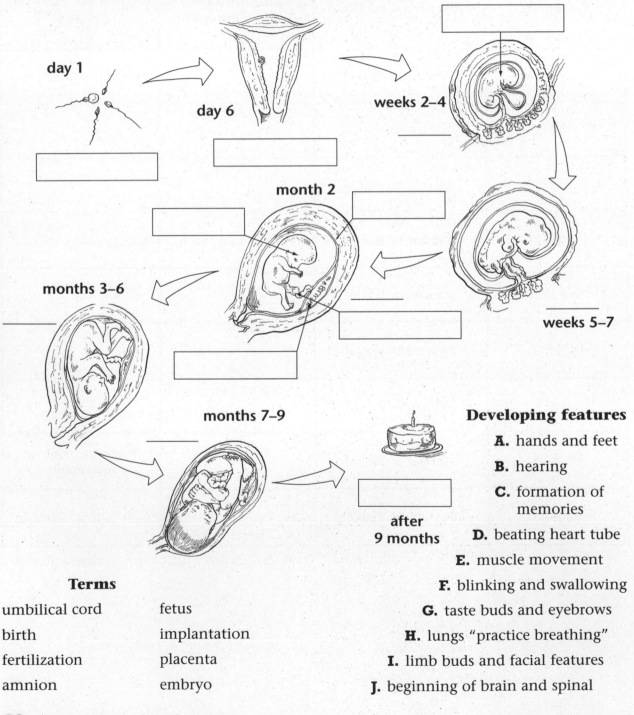

Developing features

A. hands and feet

B. hearing

C. formation of memories

D. beating heart tube

E. muscle movement

F. blinking and swallowing

G. taste buds and eyebrows

H. lungs "practice breathing"

I. limb buds and facial features

J. beginning of brain and spinal

Terms

umbilical cord	fetus
birth	implantation
fertilization	placenta
amnion	embryo

Copyright © by Holt, Rinehart and Winston. All rights reserved.

Copyright © by Holt, Rinehart and Winston. All rights reserved.

CHAPTER
26 **VOCABULARY REVIEW WORKSHEET**

A Reproduction Crossword

Complete this puzzle after you finish Chapter 26.

ACROSS

2. sexually _____ diseases pass from an infected to an uninfected person during sexual contact

4. an embryo after 8 weeks of development

7. special two-way exchange organ that provides nutrients and oxygen to the fetus and removes its wastes

9. gives birth to partially-developed live young

10. an example of a monotreme

12. connects the embryo and the placenta

16. organ where the fetus develops

17. tube inside the penis that carries semen to the outside of the body

18. organism that reproduces through budding

20. organ that makes sperm and testosterone

22. a mixture of sperm and fluids

25. a cell created from the combined nuclei of the egg and sperm

DOWN

1. a tube where sperm mix with fluids from glands

3. monthly discharge of blood and uterine lining

4. tube that leads from an ovary to the uterus

5. unable to have children

6. passageway for a baby from the uterus to the outside of the body

8. when a broken-off part of the parent's body develops into an offspring

10. temporary storage place for male sex cells

11. the time of life when sex organs mature

13. when a developed egg is released into the fallopian tubes

14. a skin-covered sac where the testes rest

15. female organs where eggs are produced

19. reproductive organ that transfers semen into the female's body during sexual intercourse

21. reproduction by combining the genetic material of two parents

23. ball of cells that must embed itself in the uterus to survive

24. produced in the seminiferous tubules

A Reproduction Crossword, continued

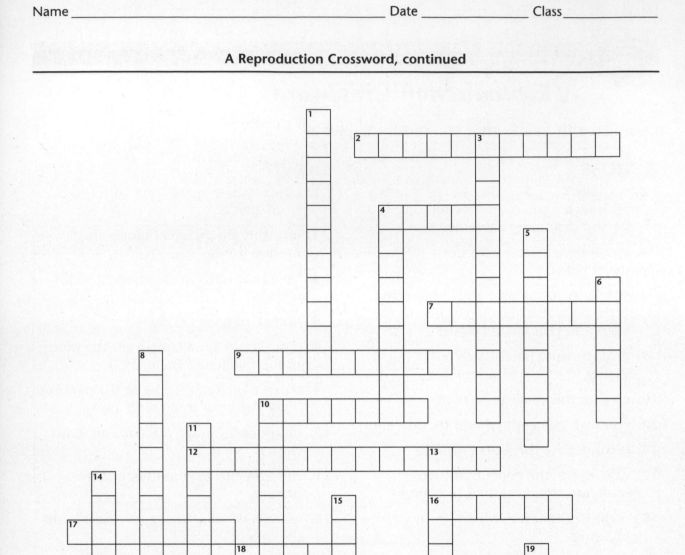

Copyright © by Holt, Rinehart and Winston. All rights reserved.

Immunity Teamwork

Complete this worksheet after reading Chapter 27, Section 2.

Your immune system works because many different types of cells work together to kill pathogens. Listed in the table below are the different cells of the immune system. Next to each of them, write a role they play in curing an infection.

Cells	How they help get rid of disease
Macrophages	
Helper T cells	
Killer T cells	
B cells	
Antibodies	

Copyright © by Holt, Rinehart and Winston. All rights reserved.

CHAPTER
27 **VOCABULARY REVIEW WORKSHEET**

Puzzle-itis Vaccine

After finishing Chapter 27, give this puzzle a try!

In the space provided at right, write the vocabulary term that best matches the clue given. Then write the circled letters in the boxes at the bottom of the page to reveal a purpose of the immune system.

1. type of disease in which the body attacks its own cells

2. kill cells infected with a pathogen

3. resistance to a disease

4. "remember" how to make antibod-ies for a specific pathogen

5. substance that kills or slows down the growth of bacteria

6. disease in which cells divide at an uncontrolled rate

7. the overreaction of the immune system to harmless antigens

8. the body system that attacks pathogens

9. cells that produce antibodies

10. special protein that attaches to a specific pathogen

11. small piece of a pathogen that generates an immune response

12. diseases that spread from one living thing to another

13. agent that causes an infectious disease

14. cells that engulf microorganisms or viruses

15. use of heat to kill bacteria in food and beverages

16. send word to killer T cells and activate B cells

A purpose of the immune system is to:

Copyright © by Holt, Rinehart and Winston. All rights reserved.

To Eat or Not to Eat . . .

Complete this worksheet after reading Chapter 28, Section 1.

Put together a balanced diet for a day. Choose one breakfast, one lunch, and one dinner from the menus below. (Assume that the portion sizes will be adjusted so you receive the correct amount of calories. Focus on selecting a balanced diet.)

Menus

	1	2	3
Breakfast	scrambled eggs bacon orange juice milk	blueberry muffin toast (with strawberry jam) orange juice milk	skip breakfast
Lunch	black bean soup pear spinach salad milk	ham-and-cheese sandwich (on rye bread) carrot sticks banana milk	cheeseburger French fries pickle soda
Dinner	spaghetti (with tomato sauce) garlic bread tofu green beans milk	sausage-and-pepperoni pizza soda	baked chicken breast rice pilaf salad dinner roll broccoli milk

1. Record the meals you chose for your healthy diet in the spaces below.

   Breakfast #_____   Lunch #_____   Dinner #_____

2. Why did you make those choices?

   _____

   _____

   _____

   _____

   _____

Copyright © by Holt, Rinehart and Winston. All rights reserved.

3. Just for fun, choose the worst diet. Again, pick one breakfast, lunch, and dinner.

Breakfast #_____   Lunch #_____   Dinner #_____

4. What problems would people who eat like this face?

_____

_____

_____

5. Some people prefer not to eat meat. Can you find a healthy vegetarian alternative among the choices? (Hint: Look at the category that includes meat in the food pyramid—it also contains nonmeat items.)

Breakfast #_____   Lunch #_____   Dinner #_____

6. What are your favorite foods for breakfast, lunch, and dinner? (There are no right or wrong answers; write down what you really like.) Write your choices in the boxes below.

Breakfast	Lunch	Dinner

7. What could you do to make your favorite meals healthier? (Hint: You can add, subtract, or substitute foods in your diet.)

_____

_____

_____

_____

8. What are water's main functions in the body? (Circle all that apply.)

  a. It transports substances.
  b. It helps regulate temperature.
  c. It provides lubrication.
  d. It breaks down fats.

Copyright © by Holt, Rinehart and Winston. All rights reserved.

Name _____ Date _____ Class _____

Hidden Health Message

After reading Chapter 28, complete this worksheet.

Circle the best answer for each question. Add that answer, next to the appropriate number, to the hidden message puzzle on the next page. The first question has been done for you as an example.

1. any substance that must be consumed to promote normal growth, maintenance, and repair

   (nutrients)   ·   minerals   vitamins

2. organic compounds that are essential, in small quantities, for good health

   nutrients   minerals   vitamins

3. inorganic elements that are essential, in small quantities, for good health

   nutrients   minerals   vitamins

4. organic compounds, composed of amino acids, that are used to build and repair body parts

   proteins   carbohydrates   cholesterols

5. organic compounds, made of sugars, that give the body energy

   proteins   carbohydrates   cholesterols

6. a type of fat known to raise blood cholesterol levels

   vitamin   unsaturated   saturated

7. a type of fat that may help reduce blood cholesterol levels

   vitamin   unsaturated   saturated

8. a disorder caused by consuming more Calories than are burned

   anorexia   malnutrition   obesity

9. a disorder resulting from consuming the wrong combination of nutrients

   malnutrition   bulimia   anorexia

10. a disorder caused by self-starvation

    malnutrition   bulimia   anorexia

11. a disorder caused by binge eating followed by induced vomiting

    malnutrition   bulimia   anorexia

12. any chemical substance that causes a physical or emotional change in a person

    drug   mineral   vitamin

Copyright © by Holt, Rinehart and Winston. All rights reserved.

13. a drug prepared from opium

    nutrient   narcotic   nicotine

14. a chemical stimulant from tobacco leaves

    nutrient   narcotic   nicotine

15. a disease in which a person is addicted to alcohol

    alcoholic   alcoholism   REM sleep

16. physical and mental response to situations that create pressure

    tolerance   stress   sleep

Hidden-message puzzle

Complete this puzzle to find out one thing you need to be healthy.

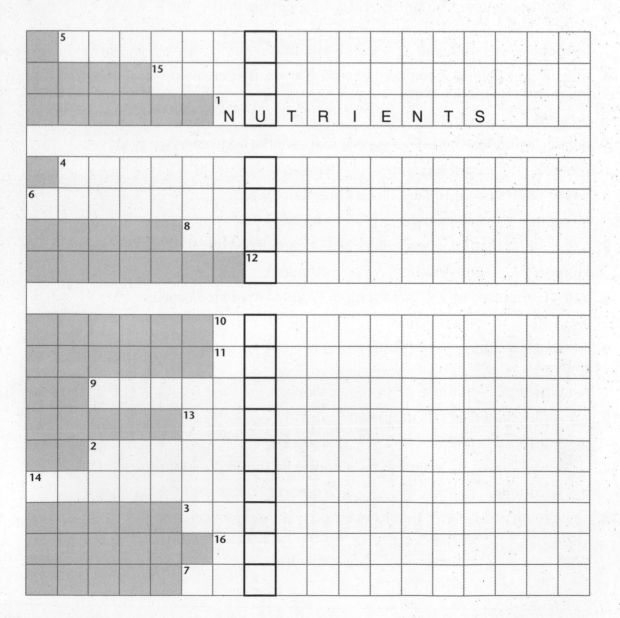

Copyright © by Holt, Rinehart and Winston. All rights reserved.

Copyright © by Holt, Rinehart and Winston. All rights reserved.

Answer Key

Reinforcement &
Vocabulary Review Worksheets

• CONTENTS •

Chapter 1: The World of Life Science 107
Chapter 2: It's Alive!! Or, Is It? 109
Chapter 3: Cells: The Basic Units of Life 111
Chapter 4: The Cell in Action 112
Chapter 5: Heredity 114
Chapter 6: Genes and Gene Technology 116
Chapter 7: The Evolution of Living Things 118
Chapter 8: The History of Life on Earth 119
Chapter 9: Classification 121
Chapter 10: Bacteria and Viruses 122
Chapter 11: Protists and Fungi 124
Chapter 12: Introduction to Plants 126
Chapter 13: Plant Processes 128
Chapter 14: Animals and Behavior 130
Chapter 15: Invertebrates 131
Chapter 16: Fishes, Amphibians, and Reptiles 133
Chapter 17: Birds and Mammals 134
Chapter 18: Interactions of Living Things 135
Chapter 19: Cycles in Nature 137
Chapter 20: The Earth's Ecosystems 139
Chapter 21: Environmental Problems and Solutions 141
Chapter 22: Body Organization and Structure 141
Chapter 23: Circulation and Respiration 143
Chapter 24: The Digestive and Urinary Systems 145
Chapter 25: Communication and Control 146
Chapter 26: Reproduction and Development 148
Chapter 27: Body Defenses and Disease 150
Chapter 28: Staying Healthy 151

Copyright © by Holt, Rinehart and Winston. All rights reserved.

Name _____ Date _____ Class _____

CHAPTER 1

REINFORCEMENT WORKSHEET

The Mystery of the Bubbling Top

MATERIALS

- small, empty, plastic soda bottle
- cold water
- plastic or plastic-foam disposable plate
- scissors
- hot water
- beaker or other container large enough to hold the soda bottle

Complete this worksheet after you finish reading Chapter 1, Section 2. Use the materials at right to conduct the activity below. Then answer the questions that follow.

1. Fill the empty bottle halfway with cold water.

2. Cut a quarter-sized disk from the plastic plate.

3. Moisten the plastic disk, and place it on top of the bottle's neck.

4. Pour hot water into the beaker until it is about one-quarter full.

5. Carefully place the bottle inside the beaker.

6. What happened to the plastic disk?

Sample answer: The plastic disk began to move on top of the bottle's neck.

_____

You just made observations.

7. Why do you think the plastic disk did that? Brainstorm for as many answers as possible. Then put a star next to the explanation you consider most reasonable.

Accept all reasonable responses. Sample starred answer: I think the plastic

disk moved because the hot water warmed the air inside the bottle.

_____

You just formed a hypothesis.

8. How could you test your hypothesis? Outline an experiment you could conduct.

Sample answer: I could try placing the bottle in a beaker of cold water to

see if the plastic disk moves.

_____

Copyright © by Holt, Rinehart and Winston. All rights reserved.

Copyright © by Holt, Rinehart and Winston. All rights reserved.

Name _____ Date _____ Class _____

The Puzzling World of Life Science, continued

1. T E C H N O L O G Y
2. T H E O R Y
3. A R E A
4. W A T E R
5. V O L U M E
6. X   R A Y S
7. C O N T R O L L E D   E X P E R I M E N T
8. P R E D I C T I O N
9. C O M P O U N D   L I G H T
10. L I F E   S C I E N C E
11. C O N C L U S I O N S
12. V A R I A B L E
13. S C I E N T I F I C   M E T H O D
14. T E M P E R A T U R E
15. M A S S
16. F A C T O R
17. M R I
18. H Y P O T H E S I S
19. E L E C T R O N   M I C R O S C O P E
20. C O M M U N I C A T E
21. M E T E R

Copyright © by Holt, Rinehart and Winston. All rights reserved.

Name _____ Date _____ Class _____

The Mystery of the Bubbling Top, continued

9. Conduct your experiment. What happened?

Sample answer: The disk did not move.

You just tested your hypothesis.

10. How do you explain the results of your experiment?

Sample answer: I think that the disk does not move because the cold

water cannot heat up the air inside the bottle.

You just analyzed the results of your experiment.

11. Do the results of your experiment match your hypothesis?
Explain.

Sample answer: Yes; if the disk had started moving as soon as it did

before, I would have known that the temperature of the water had nothing

to do with the movement of the disk.

12. Do you need to conduct more experiments to find out if your
hypothesis is correct? Why or why not?

Sample answer: Yes; there are more factors that I could change. Next, I

could change the temperature of the water inside the bottle to see what

happens.

You just drew conclusions.

Congratulations!

**You have just finished the first steps of the scientific method!
Share your results with your classmates.**

Copyright © by Holt, Rinehart and Winston. All rights reserved.

Copyright © by Holt, Rinehart and Winston. All rights reserved.

Name _____ Date _____ Class _____

REINFORCEMENT WORKSHEET

Amazing Discovery

Complete this worksheet after you finish reading Chapter 2, Section 2. Imagine that you are a biologist on a mission to Mars. You have just discovered what you think is a simple single-celled Martian organism. For now, you are calling it Alpha. Before you can claim that you have discovered life on Mars, however, you need to show that Alpha is alive.

1. What are the six characteristics you will look for to see if Alpha is alive?

a. Does it have cells?

b. Does it respond to change?

c. Does it reproduce?

d. Does it have DNA?

e. Does it use energy?

f. Does it grow and develop?

2. Outline a test or experiment to verify one of the characteristics you listed above.

Accept any reasonable answer. Sample answer: To see if Alpha responds to

change, I will present it with different stimuli, such as bright lights and

chemicals, to see if it reacts. If it does, the results will help show that Alpha

is alive. If it doesn't, I'll know that it is not alive.

3. If you can show that Alpha is alive, you will take it back to Earth for further study. What will you need to provide Alpha with to keep it alive?

I'll need to provide Alpha with the necessities of life: food (or an energy

source so Alpha can make its own food), water, air, and a place to live.

Copyright © by Holt, Rinehart and Winston. All rights reserved.

Copyright © by Holt, Rinehart and Winston. All rights reserved.

Name _____ Date _____ Class _____

REINFORCEMENT WORKSHEET

Building Blocks

Complete this worksheet after you finish reading Chapter 2, Section 3. Each of the boxes below represents one of the five compounds that are found in all cells. The phrases at the bottom of the page describe these compounds. Match each of the descriptions to the appropriate compound. Then write the corresponding letter in the appropriate box. Some descriptions may be used more than once.

Compounds in Cells

NUCLEIC ACIDS
G
K
L
N

CARBOHYDRATES
B
M
P
Q

PROTEINS
E
H
I
O

LIPIDS
A
C
D
J
Q

ATP
F
R
S

Clues

A. fat in animals
B. made of sugars
C. oil in plants
D. one type forms much of the cell membrane
E. enzymes
F. major fuel used for the cell's activities
G. "blueprints" of life

H. subunits are amino acids
I. hemoglobin
J. cannot mix with water
K. DNA
L. tells the cell how to make proteins
M. can be simple or complex

N. subunits called nucleotides
O. make up spider webs and hair
P. starch in plants
Q. source of stored energy
R. adenosine triphosphate
S. energy in lipids and carbohydrates is transferred to this molecule

ANSWER KEY

CHAPTER 2 VOCABULARY REVIEW WORKSHEET

It's Alive!

Complete this puzzle after you finish Chapter 2.

In the space provided, write the term described by the clue. Then find these words in the puzzle. Terms can be hidden in the puzzle vertically, horizontally, diagonally, or backward.

1. __stimulus__ — change in an organism's environment that affects the activity of an organism

2. __carbohydrates__ — group of compounds made of sugars

3. __homeostasis__ — maintenance of a stable internal environment

4. __starch__ — complex carbohydrate made by plants

5. __heredity__ — transmission of characteristics from one generation to the next

6. __metabolism__ — chemical activities of an organism necessary for life

7. __nucleic acid__ — made up of subunits called nucleotides

8. __consumer__ — eats other organisms for food

9. __decomposer__ — organism that breaks down the nutrients of dead organisms or wastes for food

10. __phospholipids__ — two layers of these form much of the cell membrane

11. __enzymes__ — proteins that speed up certain chemical reactions

12. __DNA__ — molecule that provides instructions for making proteins

13. __producer__ — organism that can produce its own food

14. __cell__ — membrane-covered structure that contains all materials necessary for life

15. __asexual__ — reproduction in which a single parent produces offspring that are identical to the parent

16. __lipid__ — chemical compound that cannot mix with water and that is used to store energy

17. __protein__ — large molecule made up of amino acids

18. __ATP__ — energy in food is transferred to this molecule

19. __sexual__ — reproduction in which two parents are necessary to produce offspring that share characteristics of both parents

Copyright © by Holt, Rinehart and Winston. All rights reserved.

It's Alive! continued

D	P	H	O	S	P	H	O	L	I	P	I	D	S
N	S	D	T	E	R	P	U	I	R	C	S	E	I
A	A	S	E	X	U	A	L	O	O	T	C	S	T
R	C	Y	Z	U	P	H	D	S	T	A	I	O	A
C	E	L	L	A	T	U	E	D	R	B	M	M	T
O	N	M	X	L	C	H	C	D	E	D	U	P	S
N	Z	E	H	E	C	E	Y	I	P	L	O	E	O
S	Y	O	R	I	H	A	P	L	L	U	S	E	M
U	M	N	A	R	O	L	I	S	M	Y	U	R	O
M	E	T	A	B	O	L	I	S	M	Y	U	R	O
E	S	E	R	L	N	P	R	O	T	E	I	N	H
R	H	A	M	Z	Y	T	I	D	E	R	E	H	E
A	C	E	D	I	C	A	C	I	E	L	C	U	N

Copyright © by Holt, Rinehart and Winston. All rights reserved.

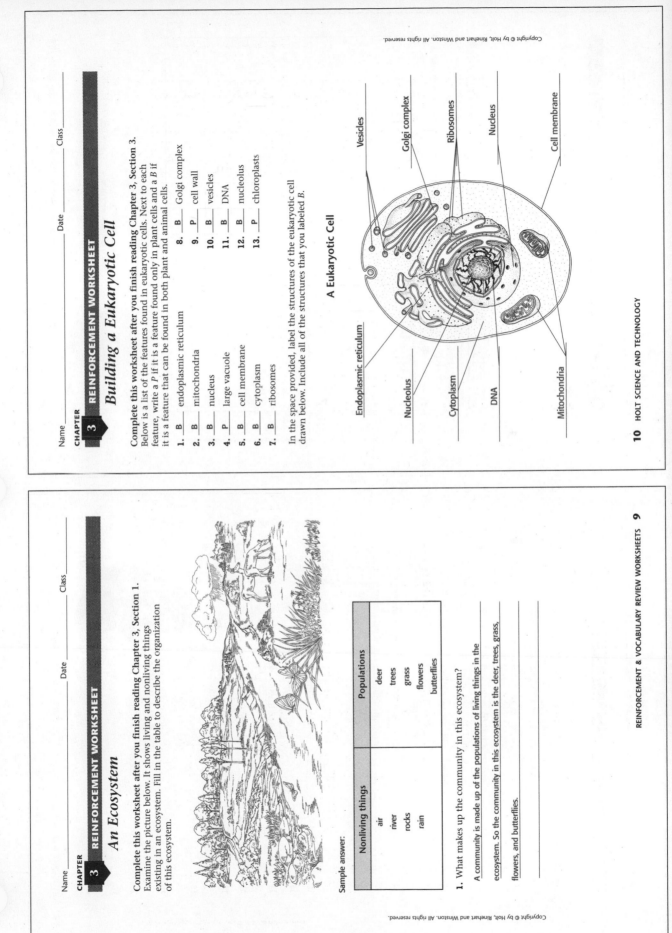

Copyright © by Holt, Rinehart and Winston. All rights reserved.

Name _____ Date _____ Class _____

CHAPTER

3 REINFORCEMENT WORKSHEET

An Ecosystem

Complete this worksheet after you finish reading Chapter 3, Section 1. Examine the picture below. It shows living and nonliving things existing in an ecosystem. Fill in the table to describe the organization of this ecosystem.

Sample answer:

Nonliving things	Populations
air	deer
river	trees
rocks	grass
rain	flowers
	butterflies

1. What makes up the community in this ecosystem?

A community is made up of the populations of living things in the ecosystem. So the community in this ecosystem is the deer, trees, grass, flowers, and butterflies.

Copyright © by Holt, Rinehart and Winston. All rights reserved.

Copyright © by Holt, Rinehart and Winston. All rights reserved.

Name _____ Date _____ Class _____

CHAPTER

3 REINFORCEMENT WORKSHEET

Building a Eukaryotic Cell

Complete this worksheet after you finish reading Chapter 3, Section 3. Below is a list of the features found in eukaryotic cells. Next to each feature, write a *P* if it is a feature found only in plant cells and a *B* if it is a feature that can be found in both plant and animal cells.

1. **B** endoplasmic reticulum
2. **B** mitochondria
3. **B** nucleus
4. **P** large vacuole
5. **B** cell membrane
6. **B** cytoplasm
7. **B** ribosomes
8. **B** Golgi complex
9. **P** cell wall
10. **B** vesicles
11. **B** DNA
12. **B** nucleolus
13. **P** chloroplasts

In the space provided, label the structures of the eukaryotic cell drawn below. Include all of the structures that you labeled *B*.

A Eukaryotic Cell

Endoplasmic reticulum

Nucleolus

Cytoplasm

DNA

Mitochondria

Vesicles

Golgi complex

Ribosomes

Nucleus

Cell membrane

ANSWER KEY

REINFORCEMENT & VOCABULARY REVIEW WORKSHEETS • ANSWER KEY **111**

CHAPTER 4 — REINFORCEMENT WORKSHEET

Into and Out of the Cell

Complete this worksheet after you have finished reading Chapter 4, Section 1. Each of the boxes below represents a different method cells use to bring small particles into the cell or to take small particles out of the cell. Add the notes at the bottom of the page to the appropriate box. Be careful—some notes can be used more than once.

Small Particle Transport

Osmosis	Passive Transport	Active Transport
particles move through cell membrane between phospholipid molecules	particles move through protein doorways	particles move through protein doorways
particles move from an area of high concentration to an area of low concentration	particles move from an area of high concentration to an area of low concentration	particles move from an area of low concentration to an area of high concentration
water	sugar or amino acids	requires ATP
does not require ATP	does not require ATP	

Notes

- particles move through protein doorways
- particles move through cell membrane between phospholipid molecules
- sugar or amino acids
- requires ATP
- particles move from an area of high concentration to an area of low concentration
- does not require ATP
- particles move from an area of low concentration to an area of high concentration
- water

Copyright © by Holt, Rinehart and Winston. All rights reserved.

REINFORCEMENT & VOCABULARY REVIEW WORKSHEETS **13**

A Cell Crossword Puzzle, continued

Copyright © by Holt, Rinehart and Winston. All rights reserved.

Copyright © by Holt, Rinehart and Winston. All rights reserved.

Copyright © by Holt, Rinehart and Winston. All rights reserved.

Name _____ Date _____ Class _____

CHAPTER
4 **REINFORCEMENT WORKSHEET**
Activities of the Cell

Complete this worksheet after you have finished reading Chapter 4, Section 2.

1. Sketch and label a chloroplast and a mitochondrion in the space provided.

2. Chloroplasts use light energy during photosynthesis. To your drawing add a light source and an arrow from the light source to the chloroplast.

3. Chloroplasts give off oxygen and glucose during photosynthesis. Mitochondria use oxygen and glucose during cellular respiration. Add this information to your diagram.

4. During cellular respiration, mitochondria produce ATP. Add this information to your diagram.

5. Besides light energy, what do chloroplasts use to make glucose?
Chloroplasts also need carbon dioxide and water to make glucose.

6. Besides ATP, what do mitochondria give off during cellular respiration?
Mitochondria also give off carbon dioxide, water, and energy during cellular respiration.

7. Add the information from questions 5 and 6 to your diagram.

Name _____ Date _____ Class _____

CHAPTER
4 **REINFORCEMENT WORKSHEET**
This is Radio KCEL

Complete this worksheet after you have finished reading Chapter 4, Section 3.

Hello, Cell-O-Rama radio fans! Katy Chromosome here. We have a very exciting program in store for you: *Cell Mitosis in Action*, with local sports announcers Sid Toekinesis and Dee Ennay. To make this a Cell-O-Rama challenge, we've spliced the sound clips from each phase of mitosis in the wrong order. Your job is to identify the correct phase for each clip and then put the clips in the correct sequence. Good luck! Dee and Sid?

Sid: Thanks, Katy. Let's roll the tape, Dee.

Dee: Rolling . . .

Segment A: Mitosis Phase _____3_____

Sid: Dee, I think the Chromatid twins are really mad this time. They seem to be storming off in opposite directions. Don't they care about the game?

Dee: This is just incredible, Sid. Wait a minute! Both groups appear to be moving into huddles. Is the game over? Do you think they'll come back?

Segment B: Mitosis Phase _____1_____

Sid: Dee, this is UN-believable. The Chromatid twins are shrinking! Are they getting ready for a fight?

Dee: Sid, I am brand new to this game, and I just don't know what might happen next. Where on *Earth* are those centrioles going?

Sid: Dee, I think things are getting too hot for them. They are hightailing it out of there.

Dee: Oh no. They seem to be throwing a net to trap the Chromatid twins. It looks like the centrioles are herding them to the center of the field.

Segment C: Mitosis Phase _____4_____

Sid: This is truly amazing, Dee. Some sort of barrier seems to be forming around each of the huddles. What is going on?

Dee: Sid, believe it or not, I think the teams are taking a timeout. See how they're all unwinding? They have worked hard today. This has been *quite* a game!

Segment D: Mitosis Phase _____2_____

Sid: Dee, maybe they're getting ready for a kickoff. The twins are lining up along the center of the field. I think they're waiting for a signal.

Dee: Sid, you can just *feel* the tension in the air. Uh oh. I think a fight just broke out. Wait—they're all *wrestling* out there! The twins look like they're trying to get away from each other. Where are the refs when you need them?

Copyright © by Holt, Rinehart and Winston. All rights reserved.

CHAPTER
5 REINFORCEMENT WORKSHEET

Dimples and DNA

Complete this worksheet after you have finished reading Chapter 5, Section 1. In humans, dimpled cheeks are a dominant trait, with a genotype of *DD* or *Dd*. Nondimpled cheeks are a recessive trait, with a genotype of *dd*.

1. Imagine that Parent A, with the genotype *DD*, has dimpled cheeks. Parent B has the genotype *dd* and does not have dimpled cheeks.

   The Punnett square below diagrams the cross between Parent A and Parent B. Complete the Punnett square. (The first square has been done for you. You may want to refer to How to Make a Punnett square in your text.)

Parent A

	D	D
d	Dd	Dd
d	Dd	Dd

Parent B

2. A Punnett square shows what genotypes are possible for the offspring of a certain cross. What genotypes are possible for the offspring of Parent A and Parent B?

Only the genotype Dd is possible for the offspring of Parent A and Parent B.

_____

3. Each of the four squares of a Punnett square represents a 25 percent probability that the offspring will have that particular genotype. What is the probability that the offspring of Parent A and Parent B will have dimpled cheeks with _____

The probability that the offspring of Parent A and Parent B will have dimpled cheeks is 25% + 25% + 25% + 25% = 100%.

_____

Copyright © by Holt, Rinehart and Winston. All rights reserved.

CHAPTER
4 VOCABULARY REVIEW WORKSHEET

Cell Game Show

After you finish Chapter 4, give this puzzle a try! This game may be played individually or in teams. You are supplied with the answers to questions in four categories. Your challenge is to come up with the correct question for each answer. Each correct "question" has a point value corresponding to the number at the beginning of the row. Keep a running total of your points as you play.

	To Make Two	On the Move	Lazy Days	I Can "C" You
50	These condense into an X-shape before mitosis.	How a cell membrane moves large particles into the cell	The movement of particles from an area of high concentration to an area of low concentration	This process ends when a cell divides and new cells are formed.
	What are chromatids?	What is endocytosis?	What is diffusion?	What is the cell cycle?
100	Human body cells have 23 pairs of these.	The movement of particles through proteins against the normal direction of diffusion	Oxygen can slip between these molecules, which make up much of the cell membrane.	This is the region where chromatids are held together.
	What are homologous chromosomes?	What is active transport?	What are phospholipids?	What is a centromere?
200	Bacteria double this way.	This word means "outside the cell."	Diffusion of water across a membrane	The way organisms get energy from food using oxygen
	What is binary fission?	What is exocytosis?	What is osmosis?	What is cellular respiration?
500	The complicated process of chromosome separation; the second stage of the cell cycle	The process by which plants capture light energy and change it into food	The diffusion of particles through special "doorways" in the cell membrane	The cytoplasm splits in two during this process.
	What is mitosis?	What is photosynthesis?	What is passive transport?	What is cytokinesis?
1000	During the third stage of the cell cycle, this forms in eukaryotic cells with cell walls.	When there's no oxygen for your cells, they use this to get energy.	Special doorways in the cell membrane are made of these.	Oxygen can pass directly through this cell part.
	What is a cell plate?	What is fermentation?	What are proteins?	What is the cell membrane?

Total Points: _____

Copyright © by Holt, Rinehart and Winston. All rights reserved.

Copyright © by Holt, Rinehart and Winston. All rights reserved.

Copyright © by Holt, Rinehart and Winston. All rights reserved.

Name _____ Date _____ Class _____

Dimples and DNA, continued

4. Parent X, with the genotype *Dd*, has dimpled cheeks. Parent Y also has the genotype *Dd* and has dimpled cheeks as well. To find out what their offspring might look like, complete the Punnett square below.

Parent X

Parent Y	D	d
D	DD	Dd
d	Dd	dd

5. What is the probability that the offspring of Parent X and Parent Y will have each of the following genotypes?

DD: 25%

Dd: 25% + 25% = 50%

dd: 25%

6. What is the probability that the offspring of Parent X and Parent Y will have nondimpled cheeks?

The probability of these offspring having nondimpled cheeks is 25 percent.

7. What is the probability that the offspring of Parent X and Parent Y will have dimpled cheeks? (Remember that there are two genotypes that can produce dimpled cheeks.)

The probability of these offspring having dimpled cheeks is 75 percent.

Copyright © by Holt, Rinehart and Winston. All rights reserved.

Name _____ Date _____ Class _____

Vocabulary Garden, continued

1. H O M O L O G O U S
2. S E X   C H R O M O S O M E S
3. A L L E L E S
4. G E N O T Y P E
5. M I T O S I S
6. H E R E D I T Y
7. M E I O S I S
8. R E C E S S I V E
9. P U N N E T T   S Q U A R E
10. D O M I N A N T
11. B R E E D I N G
12. P O L L I N A T I N G
13. S P E R M
14. P H E N O T Y P E
15. E G G S
16. P R O B A B I L I T Y
17. G E N E S

18. What do Gregor Mendel's peas have to do with the study of heredity?

Sample answer: Mendel used pea plants to study how traits are passed from parents to offspring. Mendel's results showed that each plant got two sets of instructions for each characteristic—one set from each parent plant.

Copyright © by Holt, Rinehart and Winston. All rights reserved.

Name _____ Date _____ Class _____

CHAPTER
6 REINFORCEMENT WORKSHEET

DNA Mutations

Complete this worksheet after reading Chapter 6, Section 2.

DNA is made up of nucleotides that each contain a sugar, a phosphate, and a base. The four possible bases are: adenine, cytosine, thymine, and guanine. Remember that adenine and thymine are complementary and form pairs, and cytosine and guanine are complementary and form pairs.

1. Below is half of a section of DNA that has been split apart and is ready to copy itself. Write the appropriate letter in the space provided to build the DNA's new complementary strand.

```
G -------- C
T -------- A
A -------- T
A -------- T
C -------- G
T -------- A
C -------- G
C -------- G
T -------- A
```

2. Sometimes mistakes happen when the DNA is being copied. These mistakes, or mutations, change the order of the bases in DNA. There are three kinds of mutations that can occur in DNA: deletion, insertion, and substitution.

a. Below are two sequences—an original sequence of bases in DNA and the sequence of bases after a mutation has occurred. On the original base sequence, show where the mutation has occurred by circling the appropriate base pair, and write what type of mutation it is in the space provided.

Base sequence in original cell DNA	Base sequence in a cell with mutated DNA
C G	C G
T A	T A
C G	C G
C G	C G
T A	T A
A T	A T
A T	A T
(C G)	T A
C G	
T A	

____substitution____

Copyright © by Holt, Rinehart and Winston. All rights reserved.

Name _____ Date _____ Class _____

DNA Mutations, continued

b. Below are two more sequences—an original sequence of bases in DNA and the sequence of bases after a mutation has occurred. On the original base sequence, show where the mutation has occurred by circling the appropriate base pair, and write what type of mutation it is in the space provided.

Base sequence in original cell DNA	Base sequence in a cell with mutated DNA
C G	C G
T A	A T
A T	A T
C G	C G
C G	C G
G C	G C
T A	T A
A T	A T
(G C)	A T
A T	T A
T A	

____deletion____

3. Ribosomes "read" a complementary copy of DNA in order to make proteins. Each group of three bases forms the code for an amino acid. When mutations occur in DNA, they can change the information that the DNA carries.

To understand this process better, look at the sentence below, which uses only three-letter words.

AMY GOT THE RED HOT POT OFF THE LOG

If one letter is deleted from this sentence, it can become:

AMY GTT HER EDH OTP OTO FFT HEL OG

How is this similar to what can happen when a mutation occurs in DNA?

When a deletion mutation occurs in DNA, the sequence of bases is changed and the resulting message is garbled.

_____

Copyright © by Holt, Rinehart and Winston. All rights reserved.

Name _____ Date _____ Class _____

CHAPTER 6 VOCABULARY REVIEW WORKSHEET

Unraveling Genes

Try this puzzle after you finish reading Chapter 6!
Solve the clues and unscramble the letters to fill in the blanks. Fill the letters in the squares and read the final clue to unravel the secret message.

1. Molecule that carries our hereditary information: NAD
D N A
‾ ‾ ‾
    11

2. Subunits of DNA: DISTONEUCLE
N U C L E O T I D E S
          1

3. Nucleotide base known as A: ENIDANE
A D E N I N E
16   14

4. Complement of question 3: TIEHYMN
T H Y M I N E
      5

5. Nucleotide base known as G: NUANIGE
G U A N I N E
            15

6. Complement of question 5: YOSTINCE
C Y T O S I N E
  4

7. Shape of a DNA molecule (two words): EXELLIDOBUH
D O U B L E   H E L I X
  12   7

8. Organelle that manufactures proteins: MOOSERIB
R I B O S O M E
            10

9. A change in the order of the bases of an organism's DNA: UNMATIOT
M U T A T I O N
13   17

10. Anything that can cause damage to DNA: UNGATEM
M U T A G E N
    9

11. A tool for tracing a trait through generations of a family: DEEPGIRE
P E D I G R E E
6

12. Manipulation of genes that allows scientists to put genes from one organism into another organism: (two words) NEETIEGGINGECINNER
G E N E T I C
          18
E N G I N E E R I N G

Copyright © by Holt, Rinehart and Winston. All rights reserved.

Name _____ Date _____ Class _____

Unraveling Genes, continued

13. Analysis of fragments of DNA as a form of identification (two words): PANDINGINGFRENRIT
D N A   F I N G E R P R I N T I N G
                        19

14. Genes are located on these structures that are found in the nucleus of most cells: SHROCOMEMOS
C H R O M O S O M E S
              8

15. When organisms with certain desirable traits are mated: SGEEDETRINELCVIEB
S E L E C T I V E   B R E E D I N G
        3

16. Genetic engineering is used to repair damaged: NEGSE
G E N E S
    2

FINAL CLUE:
Occurs when different traits are equally dominant and each allele has its own degree of influence:

I	N	C	O	M	P	L	E	T	E
1	2	3	4	5	6	7	8	9	10

D	O	M	I	N	A	N	C	E
11	12	13	14	15	16	17	18	19

Copyright © by Holt, Rinehart and Winston. All rights reserved.

CHAPTER **7**

VOCABULARY REVIEW WORKSHEET

Charles Darwin's Legacy

After you finish Chapter 7, give this puzzle a try.
Unscramble each of the words below, and write the word in the space provided.

1. SISEPCE — a group of organisms that can mate to produce fertile offspring

S P E C I E S

2. CATEISPOIN — the process by which two populations become so different they can no longer interbreed

S P E C I A T I O N

3. ASTRIT — distinguishing qualities that can be passed on from parents to offspring

T R A I T S

4. SVELETICE — _____ breeding is the breeding of organisms that have a certain desired trait.

S E L E C T I V E

5. TAPATIDONA — a hereditary characteristic that helps an organism survive and reproduce in its environment

A D A P T A T I O N

6. ALTRAUN — Successful reproduction is the fourth step of _____ selection.

N A T U R A L

7. GLEVITIAS — describes once-useful structures

V E S T I G I A L

8. SLOSFIS — solidified remains of once-living organisms

F O S S I L S

9. MAUTONTI — a change in a gene at the DNA level

M U T A T I O N

Now unscramble the circled letters to find Darwin's legacy.

E V O L U T I O N

CHAPTER **7**

REINFORCEMENT WORKSHEET

Bicentennial Celebration

Complete this worksheet after reading Chapter 7, Section 2.

Imagine that it is 2059—the 200th anniversary of the publication of Darwin's *On the Origin of Species*. You are a reporter for a science magazine that is publishing a special issue about evolutionary biology. Your assignment is to write an article about Darwin, his travels, and his scientific theory of evolution. Include details about the Galápagos finches and how Darwin first got the idea for his theory, and explain the steps in the process of natural selection. Don't forget to give your article an eye-catching headline!

Accept any reasonable answer. Sample answer:

_____ The Secret of the Galápagos Finches _____

In 1831, Charles Darwin, a natural scientist, traveled around the world on

the HMS *Beagle*. On the Galápagos Islands, 965 km off the coast of

Ecuador, Darwin discovered his finches. The Galápagos finches are similar to

those found in South America, but they are distinguished by the shape of their

beaks and the food they eat. Darwin theorized that the finches originally came

from the mainland but, over many generations, adapted to the different ways

the finches obtain food in the environment of the Galápagos Islands. Darwin

thought that populations of organisms change slowly over time by a process

called natural selection. The four steps in natural selection are overproduction,

genetic variation, the struggle to survive, and successful reproduction. During

overproduction, organisms produce more offspring than can survive. Some of

the offspring have different traits from each other, and this is genetic variation.

During the struggle to survive, organisms with certain traits are more likely to

survive. The organisms that survive pass on those traits to their young through

successful reproduction. Over many generations, the process of natural

selection can create a new species.

Copyright © by Holt, Rinehart and Winston. All rights reserved.

Copyright © by Holt, Rinehart and Winston. All rights reserved.

Copyright © by Holt, Rinehart and Winston. All rights reserved.

Left worksheet (page 27)

Name _____ Date _____ Class _____

CHAPTER 8

REINFORCEMENT WORKSHEET

Earth Timeline

Complete this worksheet after you finish reading Chapter 8, Section 1.
Scientists use four major divisions to talk about the Earth's history: Precambrian time, the Paleozoic era, the Mesozoic era, and the Cenozoic era. Precambrian time lasted for about 88 percent of the 4.6 billion years of Earth's history. The Paleozoic era was about 6.3 percent of Earth's history. The Mesozoic era was about 4.0 percent of Earth's history. The Cenozoic era has lasted for about 1.4 percent of the Earth's history.

The Earth's history is difficult to imagine because it is so long. But what if the entire history of the Earth could fit into a single human life span of 80 years? Fill in the timeline below to show how old a person would be when each era begins. If the first single-celled organism appeared 3.5 billion years ago, how old would the person be when the first single-celled organism appears on Earth? Indicate this on the timeline.

Age in years

0 — Precambrian time begins
5
10
15
20 — First single-celled organism appears
25
30
35
40
45
50
55
60
65
70 — Paleozoic era begins
75 — Mesozoic era begins
80 — Cenozoic era begins

On this scale, Precambrian time lasts for 70 years, the Paleozoic era lasts for 5 years, the Mesozoic era lasts for 3 years, and the Cenozoic era has lasted for 1 year.

The person will be about 20 when the first single-celled organism appears.

REINFORCEMENT & VOCABULARY REVIEW WORKSHEETS **27**

Copyright © by Holt, Rinehart and Winston. All rights reserved.

Right worksheet (page 28)

Name _____ Date _____ Class _____

CHAPTER 8

REINFORCEMENT WORKSHEET

Condensed History

Complete this worksheet after you finish reading Chapter 8, Section 2.
Many important events that have occurred since the Earth was formed are listed below. Fill in the diagram below, listing the events in chronological order.

Prokaryotes form.
Cells with nuclei form.
Began 65 million years ago
First birds appear.
Large mammals appear.
The ozone layer develops.
Dinosaurs dominate the Earth.
Plants become established on land.
Humans appear.
Crawling insects appear on land.
Many reptile species evolve.
Organisms suffer largest mass extinction known.
Small mammals survive mass extinction.
Began 540 million years ago
Cyanobacteria begin photosynthesis and produce oxygen.
Began 4.6 billion years ago
Winged insects appear.
Began 248 million years ago

Precambrian Time
Began 4.6 billion years ago
Prokaryotes form.
Cyanobacteria begin photosynthesis and produce oxygen.
The ozone layer develops.
Cells with nuclei form.

Paleozoic Era
Began 540 million years ago
Plants become established on land.
Crawling insects appear on land.
Winged insects appear.
Organisms suffer largest mass extinction known.

Mesozoic Era
Began 248 million years ago
Many reptile species evolve.
Dinosaurs dominate the Earth.
First birds appear.
Small mammals survive mass extinction.

Cenozoic Era
Began 65 million years ago
Large mammals appear.
Humans appear.

28 HOLT SCIENCE AND TECHNOLOGY

Copyright © by Holt, Rinehart and Winston. All rights reserved.

ANSWER KEY

Copyright © by Holt, Rinehart and Winston. All rights reserved.

Name _____ Date _____ Class _____

Mary Leakey's Search

Try this puzzle after you finish Chapter 8.
Solve each of the clues below, and write your answer in the spaces provided. Then complete the quotation by Mary Leakey on the next page by writing the letter that corresponds to each number in the empty boxes.

1. large mammals evolved during this era.
   C E N O Z O I C
       5 6

2. scientist who uses fossils to reconstruct what happened in Earth's history
   P A L E O N T O L O G I S T
         8 10   33 31

3. measuring the ratio of unstable to stable atoms in a rock sample to determine the age of the fossil it contains
   A B S O L U T E   D A T I N G
   24 52 28 23   17   48

4. the first true cells
   P R O K A R Y O T E S
   4 1   35   53

5. cells that contain a nucleus
   E U K A R Y O T E S
   9 30   42   56

6. scientist who discovered fossilized footprints in Tanzania
   M A R Y   L E A K E Y
   13 41   54   7

7. hominid that lived in Germany 230,000 years ago
   N E A N D E R T H A L
   16   37   51

8. an imprint of a living thing preserved in rock
   F O S S I L
   14   12

9. Lucy is the most complete example of a(n) _____ ever found.
   A U S T R A L O P I T H E C I N E
   3   36   18   32

10. When a species dies out completely, it becomes _____.
    E X T I N C T
    38 15   20

11. the theory that explains how the continents move
    P L A T E   T E C T O N I C S
    27 50 47   11

Copyright © by Holt, Rinehart and Winston. All rights reserved.

Name _____ Date _____ Class _____

Mary Leakey's Search, continued

12. a group of mammals with binocular vision
    P R I M A T E S
    49   45

13. Humans and their humanlike ancestors are called _____.
    H O M I N I D S
    46   55

14. organisms that don't need oxygen to survive
    A N A E R O B I C
      39   25

15. a gas that absorbs ultraviolet radiation
    O Z O N E
    2   57

16. the single landmass that existed about 245 million years ago
    P A N G A E A
    19   26

17. The first birds appeared during this era.
    M E S O Z O I C
    29   43

18. During this era, the first land-dwelling organisms appeared.
    P A L E O Z O I C
    40   22

19. Cyanobacteria produce this gas during photosynthesis.
    O X Y G E N
    21

20. the time it takes for half of the unstable atoms in a sample to decay
    H A L F - L I F E
    34   44

Quotation grid:

Row 1: Y O U ■ K N O W ■ Y O U ■ O N L Y ■ F I N D
1 2 3   5 6 7 8 9   10 11 12 13   14 15 16 17

Row 2: W H A T ■ Y O U ■ A R E ■ L O O K I N G
18 19 20 21 22 23 24 25 26 27 28 29 30 31 32 33

Row 3: F O R ■ R E A L L Y ■ I F ■ T H E
34 35 36 37 38 39 40 41 42 43 44 45 46 47

Row 4: T R U T H ■ B E ■ K N O W N ■ .
48 49 50 51 52 53 54 55 56 57

— Mary Leakey, 1994

Copyright © by Holt, Rinehart and Winston. All rights reserved.

Name _____ Date _____ Class _____

Classification Clues

Complete this puzzle after you have finished Chapter 9.
Solve the clues to see what words are hidden in the puzzle. Words in the puzzle are hidden vertically, horizontally, and diagonally.

1. List the seven levels used by scientists to classify organisms in order from most general to least general.

a. _____kingdom_____

b. _____phylum_____

c. _____class_____

d. _____order_____

e. _____family_____

f. _____genus_____

g. _____species_____

2. For each of the following descriptions, write the kingdom of the organisms being described in the space provided.

a. _____Eubacteria_____ Single-celled organisms without nuclei, such as *Escherichia coli*, which live in the human body

b. _____Plantae_____ Multicellular, eukaryotic organisms that are usually green and make sugar through photosynthesis

c. _____Archaebacteria_____ Unicellular prokaryotes that have been on Earth for at least 3 billion years

d. _____Animalia_____ Multicellular organisms whose cells have nuclei but do not have cell walls

e. _____Fungi_____ Multicellular organisms that have cells containing nuclei and that absorb nutrients from their surroundings after breaking them down with digestive juices

f. _____Protista_____ Single-celled or multicellular, eukaryotic organisms that are not plants, animals, or fungi

3. Linnaeus founded _____taxonomy_____, the science of identifying, naming, and classifying living things.

4. A _____dichotomous_____ key is a special guide used to identify unknown organisms.

Copyright © by Holt, Rinehart and Winston. All rights reserved.

Copyright © by Holt, Rinehart and Winston. All rights reserved.

Name _____ Date _____ Class _____

Keys to the Kingdom, continued

Animalia	Plantae
Most possess a nervous system	Usually green
Felis domesticus	Use the sun's energy to make sugar
All have cells that lack cell walls	Ferns

Protista	Fungi
Most are single-celled organisms	Break down material outside their bodies and then absorb the nutrients
All eukaryotes that are not plants, animals, or fungi	Molds
Algae	Mushrooms
Evolved from bacteria about 2 billion years ago	

Eubacteria	Archaebacteria
Escherichia coli	Have existed for at least 3 billion years
Prokaryotes that may be found in the human body	Form yellow rings around hot springs where the temperature is 90°C
All are single-celled organisms	All are single-celled organisms
Do not have nuclei	Do not have nuclei

CHAPTER 10 — REINFORCEMENT WORKSHEET

Bacteria Bonanza

Complete this worksheet after you finish reading Chapter 10, Section 1.

Complete the outline below using the following terms: *spirilla, photosynthetic, methane makers, eubacteria, decomposers, bacilli, heat lovers, consumers, salt lovers, producers, archaebacteria, parasites, cyanobacteria,* and *cocci.*

Bacteria

I. Bacteria come in three shapes:

A. ____Cocci____ are spherical.

B. ____Bacilli____ are rod-shaped.

C. ____Spirilla____ are spiral-shaped.

II. Bacteria make up two kingdoms:

A. ____Archaebacteria____ thrive in unusual places.

   1. ____Salt lovers____ are found where there is a high salt concentration.

   2. ____Heat lovers____ are found in hot springs.

   3. ____Methane makers____ are found in swamps.

B. ____Eubacteria____ get food in two ways.

   1. ____Consumers____ obtain nutrients from other organisms.

    a. ____Decomposers____ feed on dead organic matter.

    b. ____Parasites____ feed on living organisms.

   2. ____Producers____ make their own food.

    a. Some are ____photosynthetic____ .

    b. Plant predecessors may have contained ____cyanobacteria____ .

Copyright © by Holt, Rinehart and Winston. All rights reserved.

Classification Clues, continued

Copyright © by Holt, Rinehart and Winston. All rights reserved.

Copyright © by Holt, Rinehart and Winston. All rights reserved.

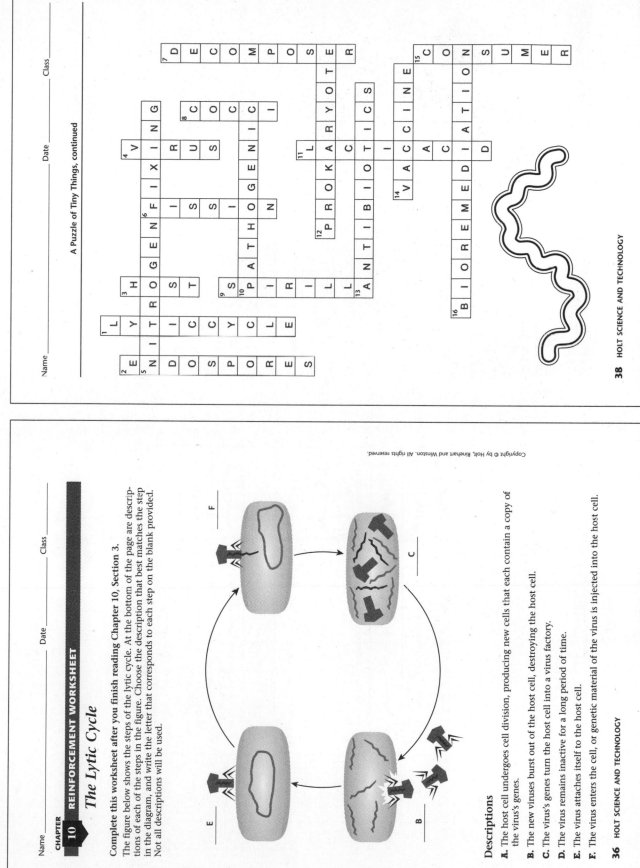

Copyright © by Holt, Rinehart and Winston. All rights reserved.

Name _____ Date _____ Class _____

A Puzzle of Tiny Things, continued

38 HOLT SCIENCE AND TECHNOLOGY

Name _____ Date _____ Class _____

Copyright © by Holt, Rinehart and Winston. All rights reserved.

CHAPTER 10 REINFORCEMENT WORKSHEET

The Lytic Cycle

Complete this worksheet after you finish reading Chapter 10, Section 3.

The figure below shows the steps of the lytic cycle. At the bottom of the page are descriptions of each of the steps in the figure. Choose the description that best matches the step in the diagram, and write the letter that corresponds to each step on the blank provided. Not all descriptions will be used.

Descriptions

A. The host cell undergoes cell division, producing new cells that each contain a copy of the virus's genes.

B. The new viruses burst out of the host cell, destroying the host cell.

C. The virus's genes turn the host cell into a virus factory.

D. The virus remains inactive for a long period of time.

E. The virus attaches itself to the host cell.

F. The virus enters the cell, or genetic material of the virus is injected into the host cell.

36 HOLT SCIENCE AND TECHNOLOGY

Copyright © by Holt, Rinehart and Winston. All rights reserved.

Name _____ Date _____ Class _____

An Ode to a Fungus

Complete this worksheet after you finish reading Chapter 11, Section 2.
A science magazine has asked your friend, the well-known poet Madeline Molde, to write a poem about fungi. Madeline started her poem, but now she has writers' block. The poem is unfinished and her deadline is tomorrow! The poem needs to be at least 12 lines long (but it can be longer) and should contain factual information about fungi. Use the terms in Chapter 11 to help Madeline finish her poem!

Fungi

Beautiful, black, fuzzy mold!
You grow in my fridge on food that is old.
Fungi! Yummy truffles that I love to eat,

Sample answer: When you are imperfect, you grow on my feet.

Most fungi eat things that are dead,

Except for the yeast that help me make bread.

Some fungi are used to make cheese,

And when I breathe them they can make me wheeze.

Mushrooms are fungi, and some taste quite good,

But others are poisonous—don't mistake them for food!

Many shapes, sizes, and colors you can be

Reproducing with your hyphae asexually!

_____

_____

_____

_____

_____

_____

_____

_____

Copyright © by Holt, Rinehart and Winston. All rights reserved.

Name _____ Date _____ Class _____

Protists on Parade

Complete the table below after you finish reading Chapter 11, Section 1.

Sample answers:

Term	Definition	Example
Parasite	invades the body of another living organism to obtain the nutrients it needs	"late blight"
Producer	makes its own food, usually by photosynthesis	brown algae
Consumer	feeds on dead organic matter or the body of another organism	scrambled egg slime mold
Flagella	whiplike structures that produce movement	*Giardia lamblia*
Cilia	tiny, hairlike structures used for movement and feeding	paramecium
Pseudopodia	structures that amoebas use to move; "false feet"	amoeba
Spore-forming	a single parent that produces small reproductive cells protected by a thick wall	*Plasmodium vivax*
Conjugation	reproduction in which two organisms join together and exchange genetic material	paramecium
Fission	reproduction in which a single parent cell splits into two identical cells	euglena

Copyright © by Holt, Rinehart and Winston. All rights reserved.

Copyright © by Holt, Rinehart and Winston. All rights reserved.

Name _____ Date _____ Class _____

A Moldy Puzzle

After you finish reading Chapter 11, give this puzzle a try!
Fill in the blanks with the appropriate terms, and then use the terms to complete the puzzle on the next page.

1. An organism that invades the body of another organism is a ___parasite___.

2. ___Imperfect fungi___ are fungi that do not fit into other standard groups of fungi.

3. ___Protozoa___ are animal-like protists that are single-celled consumers.

4. Plantlike protists that convert the sun's energy into food through photosynthesis are called ___algae___.

5. The organism that is harmed by a parasite is called the ___host___.

6. A ___lichen___ is made of a fungus and an alga that grow intertwined.

7. Any eukaryotic organism that is part of the kingdom Protista is called a ___protist___.

8. ___Thread___-like fungi include black bread mold.

9. Amoebas use ___pseudopodia___, or "false feet," to move around.

10. ___Hyphae___ are chains of cells that make up multicellular fungi.

11. The group of fungi that includes umbrella-shaped mushrooms and puffballs is called ___club fungi___.

12. A protist that obtains its food from dead organic matter or from the body of another organism is called a ___funguslike___ protist.

13. A ___spore___ is a small reproductive cell protected by a thick cell wall.

14. Fungi that reproduce by spores that develop in an ascus are called ___sac fungi___.

15. Kingdom ___Fungi___ includes complex, multicellular organisms that obtain food by breaking down other substances in their surroundings and absorbing the nutrients.

16. The major part of a multicellular fungus is a twisted mass of hyphae that have grown together called a ___mycelium___.

17. A shapeless, fuzzy fungus is a ___mold___.

18. ___Phytoplankton___ are single-celled, microscopic, photosynthetic organisms that float near the surface of the ocean.

Copyright © by Holt, Rinehart and Winston. All rights reserved.

Name _____ Date _____ Class _____

A Moldy Puzzle, continued

Search the puzzle below to find each of the terms you wrote in the blanks on the previous page, and circle these terms in the puzzle. Words may appear horizontally, vertically, backward, or diagonally.

S	M	O	M	E	T	H	R	E	A	D	O	V	E	P
R	U	R	H	O	S	T	H	E	T	A	C	I	S	I
N	I	B	O	W	I	B	L	J	E	B	L	E	I	M
I	L	R	D	S	M	S	P	O	R	E	U	F	L	P
G	C	A	L	R	N	Y	W	O	T	F	H	A	R	E
N	Y	T	A	P	H	T	P	E	A	U	R	D	F	S
U	M	O	S	F	E	O	O	H	N	C	N	E	I	E
F	N	I	P	N	K	D	P	A	Y	L	G	U	L	C
L	T	A	R	B	I	Y	L	D	O	P	I	R	O	T
E	T	H	O	T	A	L	Y	A	L	I	C	H	E	N
P	R	O	T	I	S	T	N	T	H	I	N	A	K	U
S	D	L	O	M	U	S	K	H	E	I	S	L	E	N
N	O	T	Z	A	G	N	T	F	L	U	N	G	I	G
I	N	K	O	A	N	N	O	S	A	S	A	A	N	I
Y	M	O	A	R	U	E	N	S	O	D	O	E	E	S
T	H	S	A	C	F	U	N	G	I	E	L	I	O	N

Copyright © by Holt, Rinehart and Winston. All rights reserved.

REINFORCEMENT WORKSHEET

Classifying Plants

Complete this worksheet after you finish reading Chapter 12, Section 3. Each of the boxes below represents one of the main groups of living plants. Write the descriptions given at the bottom of the page in the appropriate box. Some descriptions may be used more than once.

Nonvascular plants	Vascular plants without seeds
mosses and liverworts must obtain water by osmosis have rhizoids instead of roots usually the first plants to inhabit a new, bare environment	ferns, horsetails, and club mosses ancestors grew very large formed fossil fuels contain xylem and phloem to transport water and food

Vascular plants with seeds but without flowers	Vascular plants with seeds and flowers
gymnosperms conifers are an example seeds develop in a cone or on fleshy structures attached to branches include the oldest living trees on Earth contain xylem and phloem to transport water and food	angiosperms seeds are surrounded by a fruit are the most successful group of plants today provide land animals with almost all of the food they need to survive contain xylem and phloem to transport water and food

Notes

- ancestors grew very large
- conifers are an example
- provide land animals with almost all of the food they need to survive
- include the oldest living trees on Earth
- have rhizoids instead of roots

- angiosperms
- seeds are surrounded by a fruit
- are the most successful group of plants today
- mosses and liverworts
- usually the first plants to inhabit a new environment
- formed fossil fuels

- ferns, horsetails, and club mosses
- gymnosperms
- must obtain water by osmosis
- contain xylem and phloem to transport water and food
- seeds develop in a cone or on fleshy structures attached to branches

Copyright © by Holt, Rinehart and Winston. All rights reserved.

REINFORCEMENT WORKSHEET

Drawing Dicots

Complete this worksheet after you finish reading Chapter 12, Section 3. There are two classes of angiosperms—monocots and dicots. The main difference between the two classes is that monocots have one seed leaf and dicots have two seed leaves. However, there are other differences between them.

Below are illustrations of some of the features that distinguish monocots from dicots. Use the description of how a dicot differs from a monocot to draw the same features for a dicot.

Monocot	How is a dicot different from a monocot?	Dicot
Arrangement of vascular tissue 	A monocot has bundles of vascular tissue scattered throughout the stem, while a dicot has bundles of vascular tissue arranged in a ring.	Arrangement of vascular tissue
Flower 	A monocot has a flower with parts in threes, while a dicot has a flower with parts in fours or fives.	Flower
Pattern of leaf vein 	A monocot has leaves with parallel veins, while a dicot has leaves with branching veins.	Pattern of leaf vein

Copyright © by Holt, Rinehart and Winston. All rights reserved.

Copyright © by Holt, Rinehart and Winston. All rights reserved.

Name _____ Date _____ Class _____

CHAPTER
12 **VOCABULARY REVIEW WORKSHEET**

Those Puzzling Plants

After finishing Chapter 12, give this puzzle a try!
Solve each of the clues below, and write your answer in the spaces provided.

1. spore-producing stage of a plant
S P O R O P H Y T E
                    24

2. plants with specialized tissue to move materials from one part of the plant to another
V A S C U L A R
      3

3. male reproductive structure in a flower
S T A M E N
        12

4. dustlike particles produced in the anthers of flowers
P O L L E N
        19

5. small, hairlike threads of cells that keep mosses grounded
R H I Z O I D S
            14

6. openings in the epidermis of a leaf that let CO_2 into the leaves
S T O M A T A
          20

7. plant "pipes" that transport sugar molecules
P H L O E M
        2

8. waxy layer that coats the surface of stems and leaves
C U T I C L E
          18

9. structures that cover immature flowers
S E P A L S
5   26

10. usually obtains water close to the soil surface
F I B R O U S   R O O T
25   9

11. nonflowering, seed-producing plants
G Y M N O S P E R M S
                  8

12. part of a flower that contains the ovules
O V A R Y
1

Copyright © by Holt, Rinehart and Winston. All rights reserved.

Name _____ Date _____ Class _____

Those Puzzling Plants, continued

13. seed leaf inside a seed
C O T Y L E D O N
            11   13

14. attract pollinators to the flower
P E T A L S
          22

15. outermost layer of cells that covers roots, stems, leaves, and flower parts
E P I D E R M I S
            7

16. plants that have no "pipes" to transport materials from one part of the plant to another
N O N V A S C U L A R
          15   27

17. seed-producing plants with flowers
A N G I O S P E R M S
                    23

18. plant "pipes" that transport water and minerals
X Y L E M
        10

19. can obtain water that is deep underground
T A P R O O T
            17

20. plant stage that produces sex cells
G A M E T O P H Y T E
6   28

21. tip of the pistil; collects pollen
S T I G M A
21

22. underground stem of a fern
R H I Z O M E
            4

23. female reproductive structure in a flower
P I S T I L
          16

Write the letter that corresponds to each number in the empty boxes to form the beginning of a well-known poem.

R	O	S	E	S		A	R	E		R	E	D		A	N	D
1	2	3	4	5	6	7	8	9	10	11	12	13		14

V	I	O	L	E	T	S		A	R	E		B	L	U	E
15	16	17	18	19	20	21	22	23	24	25	26	27	28

Copyright © by Holt, Rinehart and Winston. All rights reserved.

Name _____ Date _____ Class _____

CHAPTER
13 REINFORCEMENT WORKSHEET

A Leaf's Work Is Never Done

Complete this worksheet after you finish reading Chapter 13, Section 2.
A plant makes food in its leaves. Complete the outline below by
filling in the blanks in the diagram with the words at the bottom
of the page.

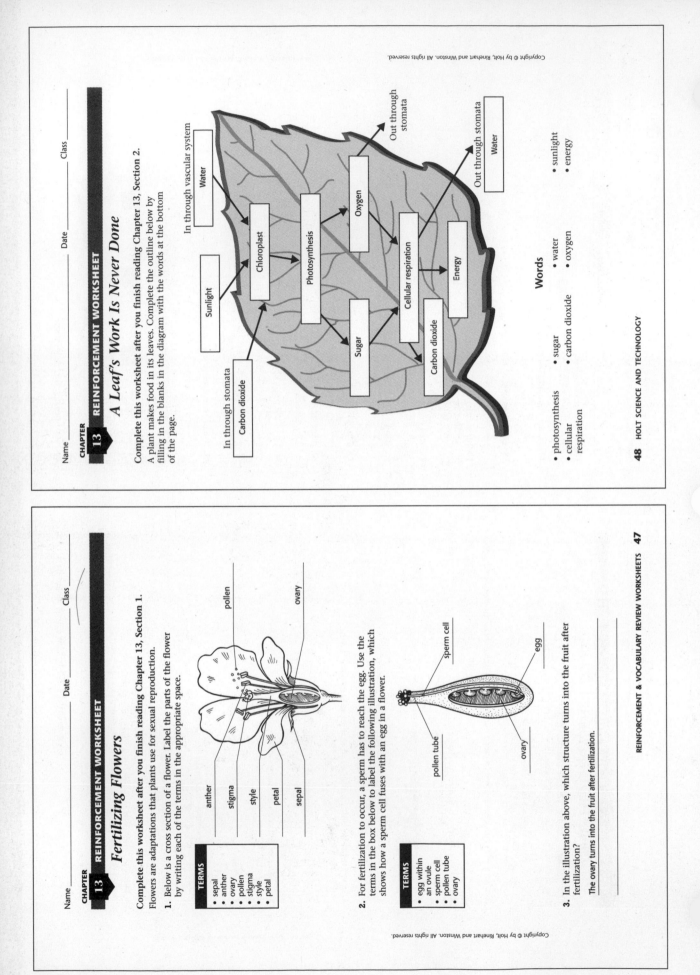

In through vascular system

Water

Sunlight

Chloroplast

Photosynthesis

Oxygen

Out through stomata

Sugar

Cellular respiration

Carbon dioxide

Energy

Out through stomata

Water

In through stomata

Carbon dioxide

Words

- photosynthesis
- cellular respiration
- sugar
- carbon dioxide
- water
- oxygen
- sunlight
- energy

48 HOLT SCIENCE AND TECHNOLOGY

Name _____ Date _____ Class _____

CHAPTER
13 REINFORCEMENT WORKSHEET

Fertilizing Flowers

Complete this worksheet after you finish reading Chapter 13, Section 1.
Flowers are adaptations that plants use for sexual reproduction.

1. Below is a cross section of a flower. Label the parts of the flower
by writing each of the terms in the appropriate space.

TERMS
- sepal
- anther
- ovary
- pollen
- stigma
- style
- petal

pollen

ovary

anther

stigma

style

petal

sepal

2. For fertilization to occur, a sperm has to reach the egg. Use the
terms in the box below to label the following illustration, which
shows how a sperm cell fuses with an egg in a flower.

TERMS
- egg within
  an ovule
- sperm cell
- pollen tube
- ovary

sperm cell

pollen tube

egg

ovary

3. In the illustration above, which structure turns into the fruit after
fertilization?

The ovary turns into the fruit after fertilization. _____

REINFORCEMENT & VOCABULARY REVIEW WORKSHEETS **47**

Copyright © by Holt, Rinehart and Winston. All rights reserved.

Copyright © by Holt, Rinehart and Winston. All rights reserved.

Name _____ Date _____ Class _____

CHAPTER 13

REINFORCEMENT WORKSHEET

How Plants Respond to Change

Complete this worksheet after you finish reading Chapter 13, Section 3.

Although plants don't walk and talk, they do respond to stimuli in their environment. Plants respond to stimuli by growing in a particular direction. Plant growth away from a stimulus is a negative tropism. Plant growth toward a stimulus is a positive tropism.

1. The plant shown below has been moved next to a window from a room with no direct light. Sketch what the plant will look like in a few days.

In a few days

2. Phototropism is a change in the growth of a plant in response to light. Is phototropism positive or negative?

   Phototropism is positive.

3. The plant shown below has just been tipped over on its side. Sketch what the plant will look like in a few days. (Hint: The plant will respond to gravity.)

In a few days

4. Gravitropism is a change in the direction of the growth of a plant in response to gravity. Is gravitropism of most shoot tips positive or negative?

   Gravitropism of most shoot tips is negative.

Copyright © by Holt, Rinehart and Winston. All rights reserved.

Copyright © by Holt, Rinehart and Winston. All rights reserved.

Name _____ Date _____ Class _____

CHAPTER 13

VOCABULARY REVIEW WORKSHEET

Scrambled Plants

After you finish Chapter 13, try this puzzle!

Use the clues to unscramble each of the words below, and write the word in the space provided.

1. IOSDDUUEC — a tree that loses all of its leaves at the same time each year

   D E C I D U O U S

2. TAOTSMA — the openings in a leaf's epidermis that allow carbon dioxide in and oxygen and water out

   S T O M A T A

3. OISRMTP — a change in a plant's growth in response to a stimulus

   T R O P I S M

4. NEREGEVER — a tree that keeps its leaves year-round

   E V E R G R E E N

5. PROLYHCHOLL — a green pigment that absorbs light energy

   C H L O R O P H Y L L

6. VAPMTGROSIIR — a change in the direction a plant grows in response to gravity

   G R A V I T R O P I S M

7. MOPTOPSIRHOT — a change in the way a plant grows in response to light

   P H O T O T R O P I S M

8. EUALCRLL EAPRRIINOST (two words) — the process that converts the energy stored in food into a form cells can use

   C E L L U L A R
   R E S P I R A T I O N

9. AAIINNTTRRSPO — the loss of water from leaves

   T R A N S P I R A T I O N

10. TRODNAM — inactive state of a seed

   D O R M A N T

Now unscramble the circled letters to find the organelle that contains the photosynthetic pigment in plants.

   C H L O R O P L A S T

Copyright © by Holt, Rinehart and Winston. All rights reserved.

Name _____ Date _____ Class _____

What Makes an Animal an Animal?

Complete this worksheet after reading Chapter 14, Section 1. Whales, armadillos, hummingbirds, spiders… animals come in all shapes and sizes. Not all animals have backbones, and not all animals have hair. So what makes an animal an animal? Complete the chart below by using the words and phrases at the bottom of the page.

Animal Characteristics

Words and Phrases

- move
- budding
- develop from embryos
- have specialized parts
- sexually
- asexually
- multicellular
- cells have no cell walls
- division
- are consumers

Copyright © by Holt, Rinehart and Winston. All rights reserved.

Name _____ Date _____ Class _____

Animal Interviews

Complete this worksheet after reading Chapter 14, Section 2. Imagine that you work with Dr. Phishtof Finz, a researcher who can really talk to the animals. Below are some sections of his taped animal interviews. Your job is to decide what animal behavior or characteristic is being described and to write it in the space provided. Possible answers are *warning coloration, migration, hibernation, estivation,* and *camouflage.*

Interviewed animal		Behavior or characteristic
Canada goose:	During the summer, we stay up in Canada. It's really a nice place in summer, with lots of food and lots of sun. But before the snow starts to fly, we high-tail it south!	migration
Arctic ground squirrel:	What's the winter like in Alaska? Strange, I really don't know. I spend all summer eating and getting my nest ready, but then during the fall I get so sleepy! I go to bed and—*poof!*—when I wake up it's spring!	hibernation
Desert mouse:	Oh, living in the desert is wonderful! I love sunshine. During the really hot part of the summer, of course, I stay inside my nest, and I nap a lot. It's so much cooler inside.	estivation
Ladybug:	Thank you! I am a lovely shade of red, aren't I? But just between you and me, did you know that this beautiful color tells birds that I am, well, rather nasty tasting?	warning coloration
Chameleon:	Yoo-hoo! I'm over here! See? In the potted plant. Well, yes, I am rather proud of being able to turn that particular shade of green. Not all animals can do that, you know.	camouflage

Copyright © by Holt, Rinehart and Winston. All rights reserved.

Copyright © by Holt, Rinehart and Winston. All rights reserved.

Name _____ Date _____ Class _____

Life Without a Backbone

Complete this worksheet after you finish reading Chapter 15, Section 1. What do a butterfly, a spider, a jellyfish, a worm, a snail, an octopus, and a lobster have in common? All of these animals are invertebrates. Clearly, there are many differences between these animals. Yet the most important characteristic these animals share is something none of them have—a backbone!

Despite their obvious differences, all invertebrates share some basic characteristics. Using the list of words provided, fill in the boxes with the correct answers. There will be some words that you will not use at all.

Characteristics

spicules
asymmetry
ganglia
gut
nerve cords
bilateral symmetry
collar cells
neutron
uniform
nerve networks
radial symmetry

All About Invertebrates

An invertebrate has a body plan that can have

_____ asymmetry
_____ bilateral symmetry
_____ radial symmetry

An invertebrate might use these structures to digest its food.

_____ gut
_____ collar cells

An invertebrate might use one or more of the following structures to control its body movement.

_____ nerve networks
_____ ganglia
_____ nerve cords

Copyright © by Holt, Rinehart and Winston. All rights reserved.

Copyright © by Holt, Rinehart and Winston. All rights reserved.

Name _____ Date _____ Class _____

Puzzling Animal Behavior, continued

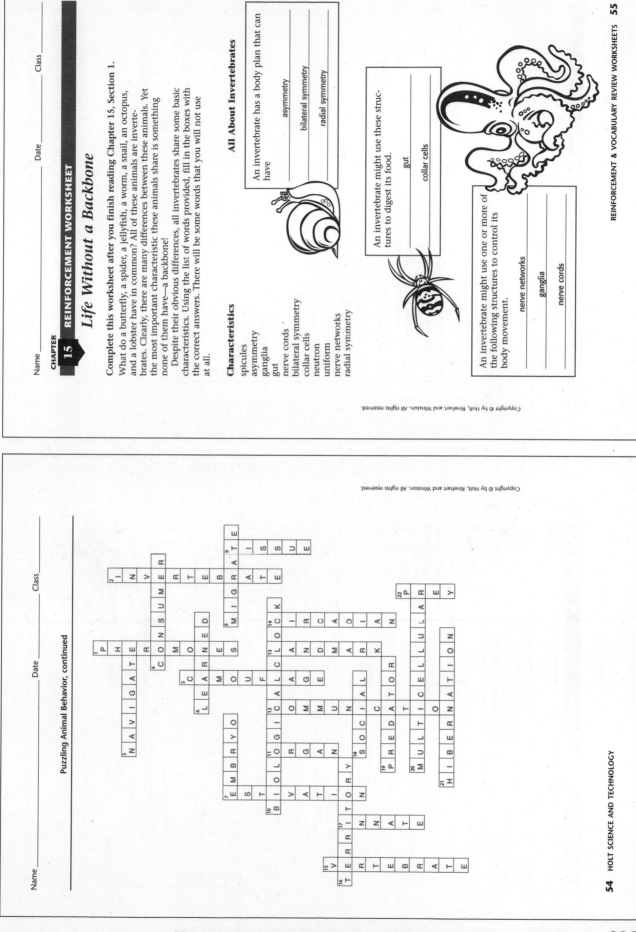

CHAPTER 15   REINFORCEMENT WORKSHEET

Spineless Variety

Complete this worksheet after you finish reading Chapter 15, Section 4.
In each of the four completed lists, seven phrases were accidentally placed in the wrong list. Those seven phrases describe Annelid Worms. Circle the phrases that were placed incorrectly in the complete the list for Annelid Worms.

Echinoderms

live only in the ocean
(have a brain)
have an endoskeleton
have a nerve ring
are covered with spines or bumps
some have a radial nerve
have a water vascular system
sand dollar
sea urchin
(a bristle worm)

Annelid Worms

have a closed circulatory system
_____

have a brain
_____

have a nerve cord
_____

have segments
_____

a leech
_____

an earthworm
_____

a bristle worm
_____

Arthropods

have a well-developed brain
have jointed limbs
have a head
have an exoskeleton
have a well-developed nervous system
a tick
(an earthworm)
a dragonfly

Mollusks

live in the ocean, fresh water, or land
have open or closed circulatory system
have a foot and a mantle
usually have a shell
have a visceral mass
have complex ganglia
(a leech)
a clam
a snail
(have segments)

Cnidarians

live in the ocean or fresh water
(have a nerve cord)
have a gut
have a nerve net
are in polyp or medusa form
have stinging cells
a jellyfish
a sea anemone
coral
(have a closed circulatory system)

Copyright © by Holt, Rinehart and Winston. All rights reserved.

CHAPTER 15   VOCABULARY REVIEW WORKSHEET

Searching for a Backbone

After you finish Chapter 15, give this puzzle a try!
Identify the word described by each clue, and write the word in the space provided. Then circle the word in the puzzle on the next page.

1. external body-support structure made of protein and chitin   _____ exoskeleton

2. combination of head and thorax   _____ cephalothorax

3. type of circulatory system in which blood is pumped through a network of vessels that form a closed loop   _____ closed

4. symmetry in which an organism's body has two halves that are mirror images of each other   _____ bilateral

5. groups of nerve cells   _____ ganglia

6. identical or almost identical repeating body parts   _____ segments

7. form of cnidarian that looks like a mushroom with tentacles   _____ medusa

8. an animal without a backbone   _____ invertebrate

9. vase-shaped form of cnidarian   _____ polyp

10. type of circulatory system in which blood is pumped through spaces called sinuses   _____ open

11. the process through which an insect develops from an egg to an adult while changing form   _____ metamorphosis

12. without symmetry   _____ asymmetrical

13. three specialized parts of arthropods formed when two or three segments grow together
  a. _____ head
  b. _____ thorax
  c. _____ abdomen

14. symmetry in which an organism's body parts are arranged in a circle around a central point   _____ radial

15. eye made of many identical light-sensitive cells   _____ compound

16. pouch where almost all animals digest food   _____ gut

17. jaws found on some arthropods   _____ mandibles

Copyright © by Holt, Rinehart and Winston. All rights reserved.

Copyright © by Holt, Rinehart and Winston. All rights reserved.

Copyright © by Holt, Rinehart and Winston. All rights reserved.

Name _____ Date _____ Class _____

Coldblooded Critters, continued

Coldblooded Critter Chart

Amphibians

- metamorphosis
- eggs laid in water
- no scales
- vertebrates
- thin, moist skin
- ectotherms
- "double life"
- breathe through skin and lungs
- external or internal fertilization
- almost all adults have lungs
- many have bright colors to scare predators

Reptiles

- ectotherms
- only internal fertilization
- amniotic egg
- most lay eggs on land
- thick, dry skin
- vertebrates
- breathe through lungs
- some have young born live
- many have scales

Fishes

- vertebrates
- mostly external fertilization
- gills
- fins
- many have scales
- many have swim bladders
- ectotherms
- lateral line system
- some have skeletons of cartilage
- some have young born live
- eggs laid in water

Copyright © by Holt, Rinehart and Winston. All rights reserved.

Copyright © by Holt, Rinehart and Winston. All rights reserved.

Name _____ Date _____ Class _____

Searching for a Backbone, continued

18. the space in the body where the gut is located **coelom**

19. an organism that feeds on another organism, usually without killing it **parasite**

20. feelers that respond to touch or taste **antennae**

21. internal body-support structure **endoskeleton**

22. organism on which the organism in item 19 lives **host**

23. system that allows echinoderms to move, eat, and breathe **water vascular**

CHAPTER 17

REINFORCEMENT WORKSHEET

Mammals Are Us

Complete this worksheet after you finish reading Chapter 17, Section 2. Each of the following terms is either an order of animals or an example of a particular order. Use the characteristics and facts in the table below to identify the order and one example of each group of animals, and record the corresponding terms in the spaces provided.

dolphin	cetaceans	hoofed mammals	sirenia
rabbit	human	carnivores	rodents
porcupine	aardvark	cow	toothless mammals
primates	manatee	Siberian tiger	
insectivores	lagomorphs	hedgehog	

Order	Characteristic	Example	An interesting fact
toothless mammals	generally eat insects and have long, sticky tongues	aardvark	only one is truly "toothless"
insectivores	tend to have pointed noses for digging	hedgehog	live on all continents but Australia
rodents	small animals that have sharp front teeth for gnawing	porcupine	front teeth never stop growing
lagomorphs	have strong legs for jumping, sensitive noses, and big ears	rabbit	some gather plants and shape them in "haystacks" to dry
primates	have eyes that face forward and opposable thumbs	human	considered the most intelligent mammals
carnivores	eat mostly meat	Siberian tiger	most have special teeth for slicing meat
hoofed mammals	generally fast runners; they have flat teeth for chewing plants	cow	divided into groups according to the number of toes
cetaceans	water-dwelling mammals that resemble fish	dolphin	use echolocation like bats do
sirenia	eat seaweed and water plants	manatee	only four species in this order

Copyright © by Holt, Rinehart and Winston. All rights reserved.

Fishin' for Vertebrates, continued

Copyright © by Holt, Rinehart and Winston. All rights reserved.

Copyright © by Holt, Rinehart and Winston. All rights reserved.

Copyright © by Holt, Rinehart and Winston. All rights reserved.

Name _____ Date _____ Class _____

CHAPTER 17 VOCABULARY REVIEW WORKSHEET

Is It a Bird or a Mammal?

Complete this worksheet after you finish reading Chapter 17.
Match each description in the second column with the correct term in the first column, and write the corresponding letter in the space provided.

d **1.** primates
j **2.** contour feathers
i **3.** carnivores
k **4.** down feathers
c **5.** gestation period
n **6.** preening
f **7.** placenta
m **8.** lift
b **9.** placental mammals
p **10.** brooding
q **11.** marsupials
o **12.** precocial chicks
g **13.** monotremes
e **14.** altricial chicks
h **15.** therapsids
l **16.** mammary glands
a **17.** diaphragm

a. a large muscle at the bottom of the rib cage that helps bring air into the lungs

b. a mammal that nourishes its unborn offspring with a special organ inside the uterus

c. the time during which an embryo develops within the mother

d. a group of mammals that have opposable thumbs and binocular vision; includes humans, apes, and monkeys

e. chicks that hatch weak, naked, and helpless

f. a special organ of exchange that provides a developing fetus with nutrients and oxygen

g. mammals that lay eggs

h. prehistoric reptile ancestors of mammals

i. consumers that eat animals

j. feathers made of a stiff central shaft with many side branches called barbs

k. fluffy, insulating feathers that lie next to a bird's body

l. glands that secrete a nutritious fluid called milk

m. the upward pressure on the wing of a bird that keeps a bird in the air

n. when a bird uses its beak to spread oil on its feathers

o. chicks that hatch fully active

p. when a bird sits on its eggs until they hatch

q. a mammal that gives birth to partially developed, live young that develop inside the mother's pouch or skin fold

64 HOLT SCIENCE AND TECHNOLOGY

Name _____ Date _____ Class _____

CHAPTER 18 REINFORCEMENT WORKSHEET

Weaving a Food Web

Complete this worksheet after you finish reading Chapter 18, Section 2.
Imagine that you are an ecologist cataloging the interactions in a salt-marsh community. Look at the illustration of some of the organisms that live in a salt marsh, and draw arrows between them to indicate how energy flows between organisms in this ecosystem.

The Salt-Marsh Ecosystem

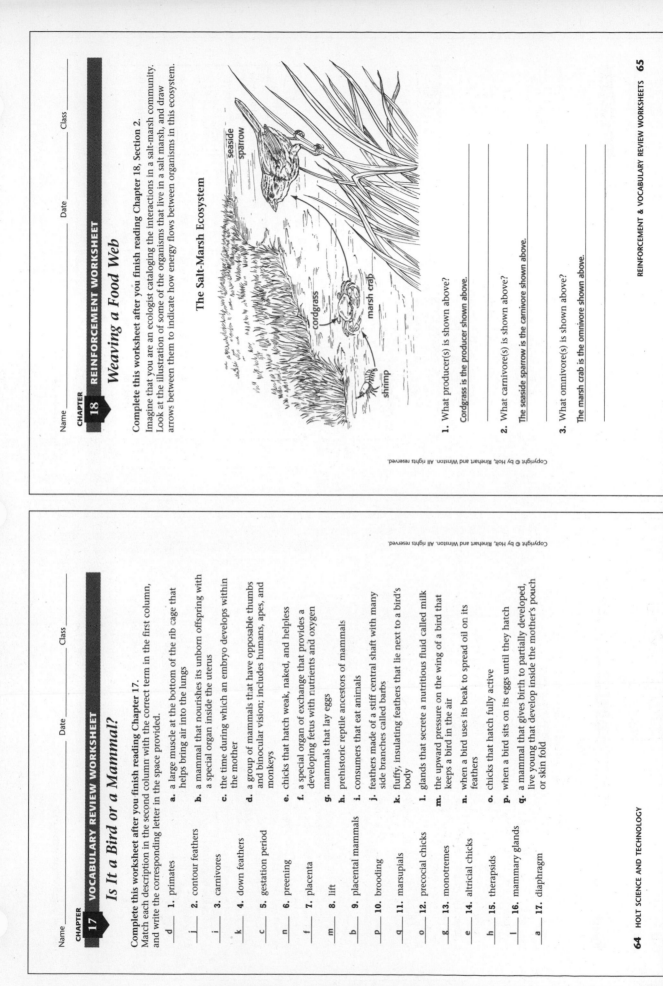

1. What producer(s) is shown above?
Cordgrass is the producer shown above.

2. What carnivore(s) is shown above?
The seaside sparrow is the carnivore shown above.

3. What omnivore(s) is shown above?
The marsh crab is the omnivore shown above.

Copyright © by Holt, Rinehart and Winston. All rights reserved.

REINFORCEMENT & VOCABULARY REVIEW WORKSHEETS **65**

CHAPTER 18

REINFORCEMENT WORKSHEET

Symbiotic Relationships

Complete this worksheet after you finish reading Chapter 18, Section 3.

In the space provided, indicate whether each of the following symbiotic relationships is an example of *mutualism, commensalism,* or
parasitism.

1. Clownfish live among the poisonous
   tentacles of a sea anemone. The clownfish
   are protected from predators, and they keep
   the sea anemone clean.   mutualism

2. Barnacles attach themselves to the shells
   of crabs. The barnacles receive a home
   and transportation.   commensalism

3. Bees use a flower's nectar for food, and
   they carry a flower's pollen to other
   flowers, allowing the flowers to reproduce.   mutualism

4. Dutch elm disease has caused mass
   destruction of elms. The fungus
   feeds on materials produced by
   the elm trees.   parasitism

5. Orchids grow in tree branches. The
   orchids receive light, and their roots
   get water from the air.   commensalism

6. Small mites live on your skin, eating
   dead skin cells.   commensalism

7. Lichens are composed of a fungus and
   an alga. The alga makes food through
   photosynthesis, and this food is used by
   the fungus and the alga. The fungus absorbs
   nutrients from the environment that are
   used by the fungus and the alga.   mutualism

8. Tapeworms live in the intestines of cats,
   where they absorb nutrients from the
   food the cats eat.   parasitism

Copyright © by Holt, Rinehart and Winston. All rights reserved.

Environmental Enigma, *continued*

1. M U T U A L I S M
2. E C O L O G Y
3. C O E V O L U T I O N
4. P O P U L A T I O N
5. H A B I T A T
6. C A R N I V O R E
7. A B I O T I C
8. C O M M E N S A L I S M
9. S C A V E N G E R
10. C O M P E T I T I O N
11. F O O D C H A I N
12. O M N I V O R E
13. C O N S U M E R
14. E N E R G Y P Y R A M I D
15. B I O S P H E R E
16. B I O T I C
17. N I C H E
18. P A R A S I T I S M
19. F O O D W E B
20. H E R B I V O R E
21. P R E D A T O R
22. D E C O M P O S E R
23. E C O S Y S T E M

Copyright © by Holt, Rinehart and Winston. All rights reserved.

Copyright © by Holt, Rinehart and Winston. All rights reserved.

Copyright © by Holt, Rinehart and Winston. All rights reserved.

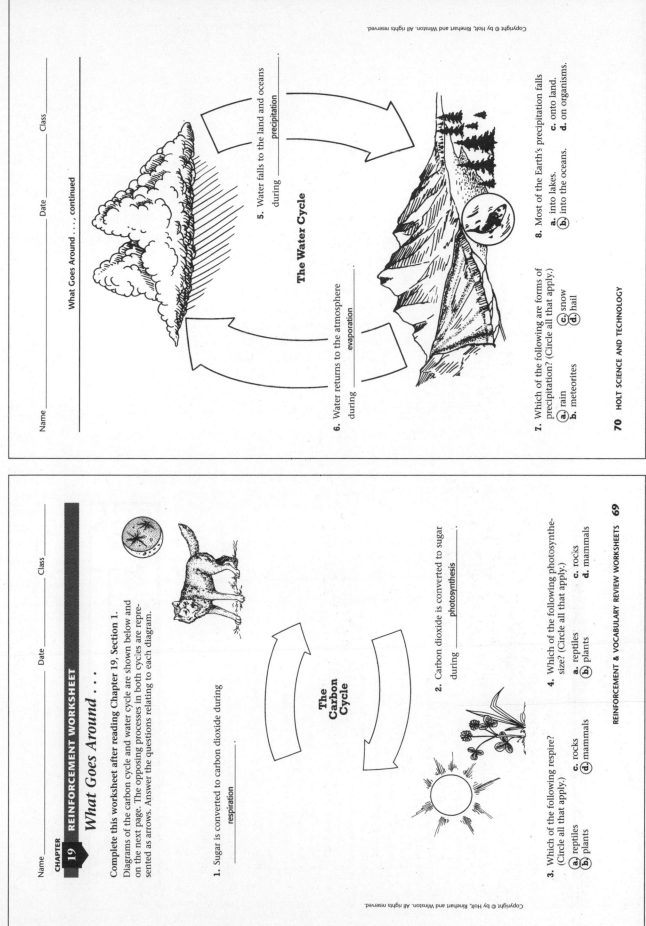

Name _____ Date _____ Class _____

What Goes Around . . . , continued

The Water Cycle

5. Water falls to the land and oceans during _precipitation_ .

6. Water returns to the atmosphere during _evaporation_ .

7. Which of the following are forms of precipitation? (Circle all that apply.)
   (a.) rain   (c.) snow
   b. meteorites   (d.) hail

8. Most of the Earth's precipitation falls
   a. into lakes.   c. onto land.
   (b.) into the oceans.   d. on organisms.

70 HOLT SCIENCE AND TECHNOLOGY

Copyright © by Holt, Rinehart and Winston. All rights reserved.

Name _____ Date _____ Class _____

CHAPTER 19   REINFORCEMENT WORKSHEET

What Goes Around . . .

Complete this worksheet after reading Chapter 19, Section 1.
Diagrams of the carbon cycle and water cycle are shown below and on the next page. The opposing processes in both cycles are represented as arrows. Answer the questions relating to each diagram.

The Carbon Cycle

1. Sugar is converted to carbon dioxide during _respiration_ .

2. Carbon dioxide is converted to sugar during _photosynthesis_ .

3. Which of the following respire? (Circle all that apply.)
   (a.) reptiles   c. rocks
   (b.) plants   (d.) mammals

4. Which of the following photosynthesize? (Circle all that apply.)
   a. reptiles   c. rocks
   (b.) plants   d. mammals

REINFORCEMENT & VOCABULARY REVIEW WORKSHEETS 69

Copyright © by Holt, Rinehart and Winston. All rights reserved.

ANSWER KEY

Copyright © by Holt, Rinehart and Winston. All rights reserved.

Name _____ Date _____ Class _____

Cycle Search, continued

S	K	S	J	W	O	D	P	G	U	Y	H	C	A	E	Q	T	F	M	X	I
B	E	L	I	N	S	G	D	N	I	T	R	O	G	E	N	C	Y	C	L	E
H	I	C	J	K	W	R	U	V	W	O	Q	D	B	B	A	N	A	N	A	N
M	P	I	O	N	E	E	R	S	P	E	C	I	E	S	P	O	O	O	G	
A	E	C	F	N	E	Y	N	I	E	T	O	R	P	L	N	I	R	I	S	T
G	R	O	U	N	D	W	A	T	E	R	V	I	C	H	S	T	T	K	B	
X	Y	M	I	O	Q	A	J	D	R	E	V	W	I	S	R	A	M	I	F	G
T	A	B	L	T	S	R	E	M	A	T	T	E	R	T	R	H	S	S	X	
R	C	U	K	T	S	A	E	Y	N	L	A	C	V	I	L	I	P	O	Y	I
O	B	S	A	T	I	N	M	E	S	O	C	U	P	Q	I	P	U	P	P	Y
W	A	T	E	R	C	Y	C	L	E	U	H	I	D	O	J	S	A	M	E	X
F	G	I	R	U	K	H	R	O	S	I	C	K	B	E	D	E	S	O	T	O
M	M	O	A	B	G	I	R	Y	L	E	Y	C	P	S	I	R	H	C	V	X
C	S	N	T	U	K	F	R	I	R	B	E	Y	E	B	S	I	A	E	X	S
G	R	O	U	P	Q	A	D	P	S	H	Y	N	O	S	A	L	A	D	J	L
M	B	I	O	T	M	U	S	T	S	U	C	C	E	S	S	I	O	N	V	W
X	F	E	N	I	T	R	O	G	E	N	F	I	X	A	T	I	O	N	N	O
C	C	A	R	B	O	N	C	Y	C	L	E	A	U	Q	E	H	O	D	T	P
J	K	P	L	I	P	Y	K	I	W	D	G	N	U	P	R	H	I	N	E	J

Name _____ Date _____ Class _____

Cycle Search

After reading Chapter 19, give this puzzle a try!
The clues on this page will help you find the words in the puzzle on the next page. Write the answers next to the clues and circle the words in the puzzle.

1. water located within the rocks below the Earth's surface — ground water

2. anything that has volume and mass — matter

3. the burning of fuel — combustion

4. the development of a community where no life had existed before — primary succession

5. the process of changing atmospheric nitrogen into forms that plants can use — nitrogen fixation

6. Sugar molecules are broken down to release energy. — respiration

7. the movement of carbon through the environment and living things — carbon cycle

8. water, in solid or liquid form, that falls from the atmosphere to the Earth — precipitation

9. the movement of water among the oceans, atmosphere, land, and living things — water cycle

10. the ecological development of a community — succession

11. the breakdown of dead materials — decomposition

12. the movement of nitrogen through the environment and living organisms — nitrogen cycle

13. the redevelopment of a community after an ecological disturbance — secondary succession

14. the first species to colonize a lifeless area — pioneer species

Copyright © by Holt, Rinehart and Winston. All rights reserved.

Copyright © by Holt, Rinehart and Winston. All rights reserved.

Copyright © by Holt, Rinehart and Winston. All rights reserved.

Name _____ Date _____ Class _____

Know Your Biomes, continued

Type of biome	Temperature & rainfall	Examples & characteristics
arctic tundra	summer: 12°C winter: −26°C rain: 30–50 cm per year	has no trees permafrost musk ox
coniferous forest	summer: 14°C winter: −10°C rain: 35–75 cm per year	waxy coating on needles trees produce seed in cones porcupine
temperate grassland	summer: 30°C winter: 0°C rain: 25–75 cm per year	has few slow-growing plants very few trees bison

EXAMPLES AND CHARACTERISTICS

musk ox
bison
giraffe
woodpecker
porcupine
animals prefer life in the treetops
most animals are active at night
trees produce seeds in cones
very few trees
plants spaced far apart
permafrost
trees lose leaves in fall
diverse groups of herbivores live here
most nutrients in the vegetation

74 HOLT SCIENCE AND TECHNOLOGY

Name _____ Date _____ Class _____

Know Your Biomes

Complete this worksheet after you have finished reading Chapter 20, Section 1.

1. Using the Temperature & rainfall column as a guide, label the biomes using the following terms: *desert, tropical rain forest, arctic tundra, coniferous forest, temperate grassland, savanna,* and *temperate deciduous forest.*

2. Use the examples and characteristics given in the box on the next page to fill in the appropriate blanks.

Type of biome	Temperature & rainfall	Examples & characteristics
desert	summer: 38°C winter: 7°C rain: less than 25 cm per year	jack rabbit most animals are active at night plants spaced far apart
savanna	dry season: 34°C wet season: 16°C rain: 150 cm per year	has scattered clumps of trees diverse groups of herbivores live here giraffe
tropical rain forest	daytime: 34°C nighttime: 20°C rain: up to 400 cm per year	the most biologically diverse biome animals prefer life in the treetops most nutrients in the vegetation
temperate deciduous forest	summer: 28°C winter: 6°C rain: 75–125 cm per year	woody shrubs beneath tree layer woodpecker trees lose leaves in fall

Copyright © by Holt, Rinehart and Winston. All rights reserved.

REINFORCEMENT & VOCABULARY REVIEW WORKSHEETS 73

CHAPTER
20 **VOCABULARY REVIEW WORKSHEET**

Eco-Puzzle

After you finish Chapter 20, give this puzzle a try!
In the space provided, write the term described by the clue. Then find those words in the puzzle. Terms can be hidden in the puzzle vertically, horizontally, diagonally, or backward.

1. a biome in the far north where no trees can grow
   __tundra__

2. a tree that produces seeds in a cone   __conifer__

3. soil that is always frozen   __permafrost__

4. a hot, dry biome that receives less than 25 cm of rain a year
   __desert__

5. the zone of a lake or pond closest to the edge of the land
   __littoral__

6. a treeless wetland ecosystem   __marsh__

7. microscopic photosynthetic organisms in the ocean
   __phytoplankton__

8. geographic area characterized by certain types of plants and
   animals   __biome__

9. trees that lose their leaves in the fall
   __deciduous__

10. a wetland ecosystem with trees   __swamp__

11. an algae that forms rafts in the Sargasso Sea
    __Sargassum__

12. an area where fresh and salty waters constantly mix
    __estuary__

13. land where the water level is near or above the surface of the
    ground for most of the year   __wetland__

14. very small consumers in the ocean   __zooplankton__

15. a tropical grassland with scattered clumps of trees
    __savanna__

16. a small stream or river that flows into a larger one
    __tributary__

17. nonliving factors in the environment
    __abiotic__

Copyright © by Holt, Rinehart and Winston. All rights reserved.

Eco-Puzzle, continued

18. a measure of the number of species an area contains
    __diversity__

T	S	O	N	O	D	E	S	E	R	T	A	R	I	N	Z	X
U	V	C	W	T	R	I	B	U	E	Z	P	C	H	O	V	G
N	B	Q	E	F	E	G	C	L	I	T	T	O	R	A	L	L
D	L	S	T	S	O	R	F	A	M	R	E	P	Q	U	L	B
R	H	A	L	P	E	M	A	F	P	O	L	N	B	K	S	C
A	O	V	A	R	C	X	S	A	R	A	O	J	T	W	G	F
P	Y	D	N	D	V	F	J	C	N	T	G	O	A	Y	E	D
H	R	I	D	E	A	R	W	K	K	Y	N	M	C	M	H	S
Y	A	V	R	C	L	S	T	N	B	L	P	Z	O	X	L	A
T	U	E	M	I	Q	O	A	G	Q	C	I	N	K	Z	N	N
O	T	R	Y	D	N	L	P	R	M	O	B	T	I	R	O	N
P	S	S	C	U	P	I	B	E	G	K	F	V	F	Q	O	A
Z	E	I	Q	O	M	W	E	T	L	A	T	B	E	J	P	V
A	G	T	U	N	D	L	F	D	O	S	G	R	L	L	A	O
I	W	Y	R	S	C	I	T	O	I	B	A	S	O	N	B	S
V	H	E	A	B	M	A	R	S	H	N	D	L	U	W	T	E
P	D	J	L	C	Y	R	A	T	U	B	I	R	T	M	N	V

Copyright © by Holt, Rinehart and Winston. All rights reserved.

Copyright © by Holt, Rinehart and Winston. All rights reserved.

Name _____ Date _____ Class _____

Solve the Environmental Puzzle, continued

1. B I O D E G R A D A B L E
2. R E S O U R C E   R E C O V E R Y
3. R A D I O A C T I V E
4. O V E R P O P U L A T I O N
5. R E C Y C L I N G
6. D E F O R E S T A T I O N
7. E N V I R O N M E N T
8. A L I E N
9. P O L L U T A N T S
10. H A L F A   A L D O R A S L
11. R E N E W A B L E
12. N O N R E N E W A B L E
13. P E S T I C I D E S
14. C O N S E R V A T I O N
15. B I O D I V E R S I T Y
16. T O X I C
17. P O L L U T I O N
18. O Z O N E

Name _____ Date _____ Class _____

CHAPTER 22

REINFORCEMENT WORKSHEET

The Hipbone's Connected to the . . .

Complete this worksheet after you finish reading Chapter 22, Section 2. Your skeleton makes it possible for you to move. It provides your organs with protection, stores minerals, makes white and red blood cells, and supports your body. Look at the human skeleton below, and write the names of the major bones listed below in the spaces provided.

Bones

- humerus
- fibula
- pelvic girdle
- radius
- patella
- ulna
- ribs
- skull
- clavicle
- vertebral column
- femur
- tibia

[Skeleton diagram with labels: skull, clavicle, ribs, humerus, vertebral column, radius, ulna, femur, patella, tibia, pelvic girdle, fibula]

The place where two or more bones connect is called a joint. In the chapter, you looked at fixed, ball-and-socket, and hinge joints.

1. What kind of joint is the elbow?

   The elbow is a hinge joint.

2. What kind of joint allows the arm to move freely in all directions?

   A ball-and-socket joint, the shoulder, allows the arm to move freely in all directions.

Copyright © by Holt, Rinehart and Winston. All rights reserved.

ANSWER KEY

Page 84 (A Connective Crossword, continued)

Name _____ Date _____ Class _____

A Connective Crossword, continued

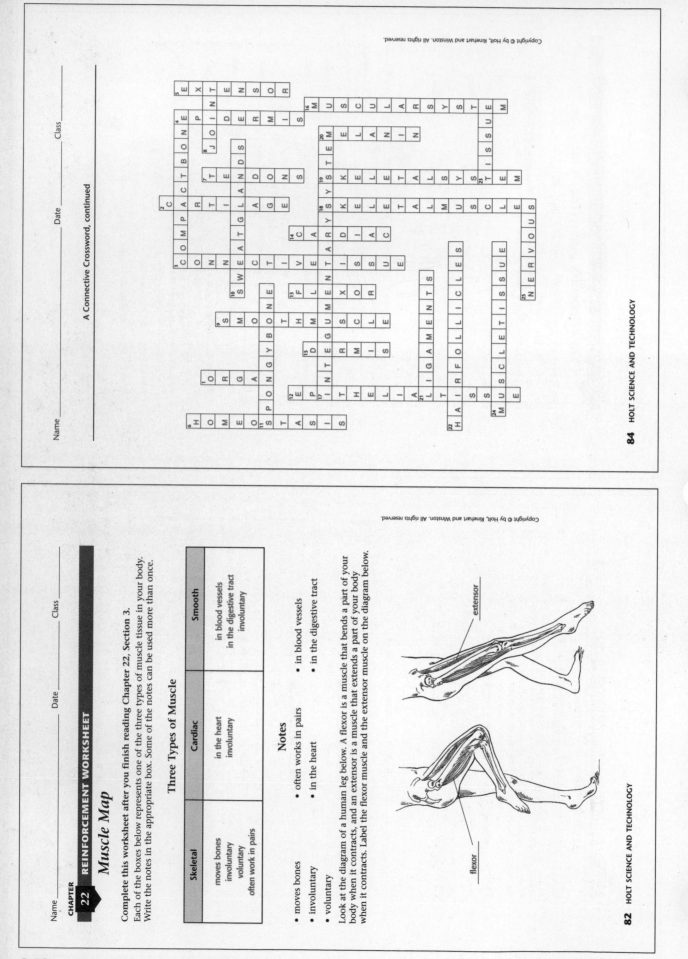

Copyright © by Holt, Rinehart and Winston. All rights reserved.

Page 82 (Muscle Map)

Name _____ Date _____ Class _____

Muscle Map

Complete this worksheet after you finish reading Chapter 22, Section 3.

Each of the boxes below represents one of the three types of muscle tissue in your body. Write the notes in the appropriate box. Some of the notes can be used more than once.

Three Types of Muscle

Skeletal	Cardiac	Smooth
moves bones involuntary voluntary often work in pairs	in the heart involuntary	in blood vessels in the digestive tract involuntary

Notes

- moves bones
- involuntary
- voluntary
- often works in pairs
- in the heart
- in blood vessels
- in the digestive tract

Look at the diagram of a human leg below. A flexor is a muscle that bends a part of your body when it contracts, and an extensor is a muscle that extends a part of your body when it contracts. Label the flexor muscle and the extensor muscle on the diagram below.

extensor

flexor

Copyright © by Holt, Rinehart and Winston. All rights reserved.

Copyright © by Holt, Rinehart and Winston. All rights reserved.

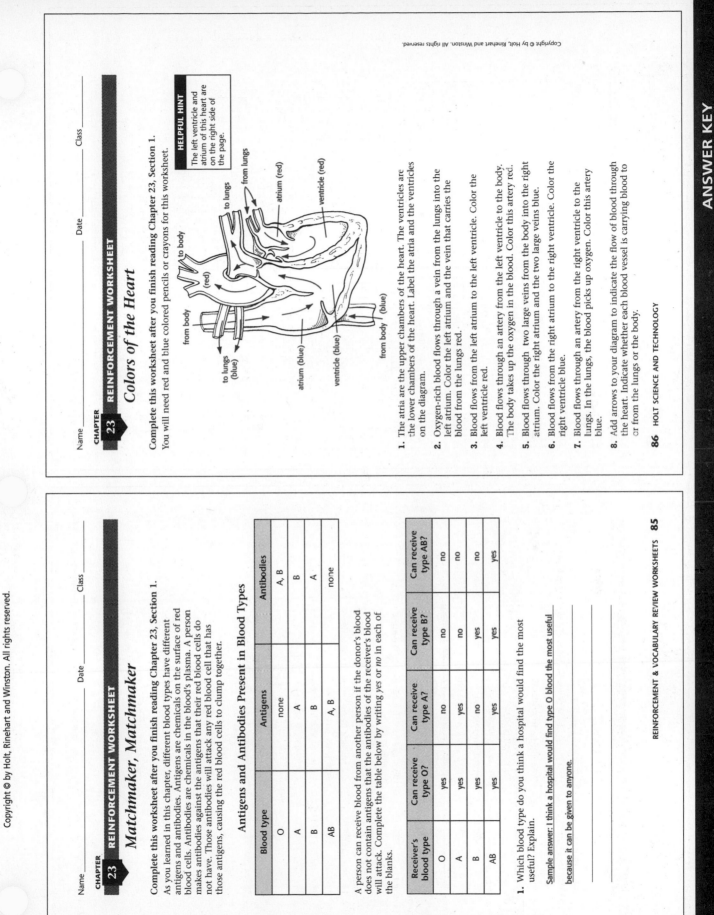

Name _____ Date _____ Class _____

Copyright © by Holt, Rinehart and Winston. All rights reserved.

CHAPTER 23

REINFORCEMENT WORKSHEET

Matchmaker, Matchmaker

Complete this worksheet after you finish reading Chapter 23, Section 1.

As you learned in this chapter, different blood types have different antigens and antibodies. Antigens are chemicals on the surface of red blood cells. Antibodies are chemicals in the blood's plasma. A person makes antibodies against the antigens that their red blood cells do not have. Those antibodies will attack any red blood cell that has those antigens, causing the red blood cells to clump together.

Antigens and Antibodies Present in Blood Types

Blood type	Antigens	Antibodies
O	none	A, B
A	A	B
B	B	A
AB	A, B	none

A person can receive blood from another person if the donor's blood does not contain antigens that the antibodies of the receiver's blood will attack. Complete the table below by writing *yes* or *no* in each of the blanks.

Receiver's blood type	Can receive type O?	Can receive type A?	Can receive type B?	Can receive type AB?
O	yes	no	no	no
A	yes	yes	no	no
B	yes	no	yes	no
AB	yes	yes	yes	yes

1. Which blood type do you think a hospital would find the most useful? Explain.

   <u>Sample answer: I think a hospital would find type O blood the most useful</u>

   <u>because it can be given to anyone.</u>

Copyright © by Holt, Rinehart and Winston. All rights reserved.

REINFORCEMENT & VOCABULARY REVIEW WORKSHEETS **85**

Name _____ Date _____ Class _____

Copyright © by Holt, Rinehart and Winston. All rights reserved.

CHAPTER 23

REINFORCEMENT WORKSHEET

Colors of the Heart

Complete this worksheet after you finish reading Chapter 23, Section 1. You will need red and blue colored pencils or crayons for this worksheet.

HELPFUL HINT

The left ventricle and atrium of this heart are on the right side of the page.

to lungs

to body (red)

from body (red)

atrium (red)

ventricle (red)

to lungs (blue)

atrium (blue)

ventricle (blue)

from lungs

from body (blue)

1. The atria are the upper chambers of the heart. The ventricles are the lower chambers of the heart. Label the atria and the ventricles on the diagram.

2. Oxygen-rich blood flows through a vein from the lungs into the left atrium. Color the left atrium and the vein that carries the blood from the lungs red.

3. Blood flows from the left atrium to the left ventricle. Color the left ventricle red.

4. Blood flows through an artery from the left ventricle to the body. The body takes up the oxygen in the blood. Color this artery red.

5. Blood flows through two large veins from the body into the right atrium. Color the right atrium and the two large veins blue.

6. Blood flows from the right atrium to the right ventricle. Color the right ventricle blue.

7. Blood flows through an artery from the right ventricle to the lungs. In the lungs, the blood picks up oxygen. Color this artery blue.

8. Add arrows to your diagram to indicate the flow of blood through the heart. Indicate whether each blood vessel is carrying blood to or from the lungs or the body.

86 HOLT SCIENCE AND TECHNOLOGY

Copyright © by Holt, Rinehart and Winston. All rights reserved.

Name _____ Date _____ Class _____

A Hunt with Heart, continued

21. _____ respiratory — this system consists of the lungs, the throat, and the passageways that lead to the lungs

22. _____ ventricles — lower heart chambers

23. _____ veins — blood vessels that direct blood toward the heart

24. _____ alveoli — tiny sacs that form the bronchiole branches of the lungs

25. _____ trachea — your windpipe

26. _____ bronchi — the two tubes that connect the lungs with the trachea

How many chapter concepts can you find in the block of letters below? Use the clues to help you find them. Words may appear horizontally, vertically, diagonally, or backward.

G	L	Y	M	P	H	A	T	I	C	I	M	E	T	S	Y	S	A
T	I	A	L	V	E	O	L	I	T	O	L	N	M	O	V	L	O
O	B	S	U	R	D	S	H	U	O	C	T	E	F	O	S	Y	S
N	E	L	A	O	E	C	P	A	B	C	A	C	L	Q	Y	M	C
S	H	T	O	I	N	T	H	Y	T	A	P	L	I	M	R	P	A
I		L	R	O	X	Y	L	N	D	R	X	N	Y	R	A	H	P
L	B	A	R	O	D	D	T	B	I	D	I	T	R	E	N	N	I
S	Y	B	L	B	I	P	C	Y	G	I	S	A	O	S	O	O	L
E	B	M	A	R	A	L	R	S	U	O	B	O	T	P	M	D	L
L	M	L	P	R	P	A	H	E	E	V	I	X	A	I	L	E	A
C	A	H	G	H	T	U	I	S	A	R	L	R	R	U	S	S	R
I	W	R	O	R	R	E	S	R	P	S	D	T	I	A	P	U	I
R	X	N	Y	R	A	L	E	L	E	L	C	U	B	P	T	J	M
T	C	T	V	S	G	E	Y	T	E	U	P	R	S	I	E	U	S
N	C	A	N	D	M	T	K	R	E	L	I	E	E	O	S	S	R
E	P	E	P	L	A	S	M	A	N	A	Y	M	R	N	T	E	I
V	E	I	N	S	U	M	Y	H	T	R	A	C	H	E	A	Z	N

Name _____ Date _____ Class _____

A Hunt with Heart

After finishing Chapter 23, give this puzzle a try!
Solve the clues below. Then use the clues to complete the puzzle on the next page.

1. _____ cardiovascular — system that transports materials to and from the body's cells

2. _____ blood — a connective tissue made up of cells, cell parts, and plasma

3. _____ plasma — the fluid part of blood

4. _____ spleen — largest lymph organ

5. _____ pharynx — upper portion of the throat

6. _____ lymphatic — system that collects extracellular fluid and returns it to your blood

7. _____ thymus — lymph organ just above the heart that produces lymphocytes

8. _____ lymph — fluid and particles absorbed into lymph capillaries

9. _____ pulmonary — type of blood circulation between the heart and the lungs

10. _____ capillaries — the smallest blood vessels in the body

11. _____ larynx — your voice box

12. _____ blood pressure — expressed in millimeters of Mercury (mm Hg)

13. _____ platelets — cell fragments that clump together to form a plug that helps reduce blood loss

14. _____ lymph nodes — small bean-shaped organs that remove particles from lymph

15. _____ respiration — process that is made up of breathing and cellular respiration

16. _____ systemic — type of blood circulation between the heart and the rest of the body

17. _____ diaphragm — dome-shaped muscle involved in breathing

18. _____ atria — upper heart chambers

19. _____ arteries — blood vessels that direct blood away from the heart

20. _____ tonsils — made up of groups of lymphatic tissue located inside your throat, at the back of your nasal cavity, and at the back of your tongue

Copyright © by Holt, Rinehart and Winston. All rights reserved.

Copyright © by Holt, Rinehart and Winston. All rights reserved.

Copyright © by Holt, Rinehart and Winston. All rights reserved.

Name _____ Date _____ Class _____

Annie Apple's Amazing Adventure

Complete this worksheet after you finish reading Chapter 24, Section 2. Being an apple, Annie is just not very good with words. In her story below she used many terms incorrectly. The incorrect terms have been underlined and numbered. Help Annie by writing the correct term in the corresponding blank provided at the bottom of the page.

> Hi, my name is Annie Apple, and I'm, well, an apple! I've just been on the strangest adventure, and I thought you'd like to hear about it.
>
> First, this girl took a huge bite out of me and used her teeth to chew me. They call that (1) chemical digestion. While this was happening I got soaked by (2) bile, which breaks down my carbohydrates into simple sugars. Boy, was that uncomfortable! Then I was swallowed.
>
> I went down a long tube called the (3) small intestine, and I ended up in the (4) liver. There, I was bombarded by acid and enzymes, which broke me down further until I was a soupy mixture called (5) anus. Next, I was released into the (6) large intestine. There I was met by pancreatic juice and (7) saliva. Then I was broken down enough to be partially absorbed into the bloodstream.
>
> After that, I passed into the (8) esophagus, where I had water absorbed from me. At last, what was left of me passed through an opening called the (9) villi. But that's not the end! The part of me that passed into the bloodstream provided energy to lots of cells before it ended up at the (10) stomach, where it was filtered through tiny (11) bladders and then went out the (12) urethra to be stored in the (13) nephron.
>
> The final leg of my journey was through the (14) ureter to the outside world. Isn't that an unbelievable adventure?

1. mechanical digestion
2. saliva
3. esophagus
4. stomach
5. chyme
6. small intestine
7. bile
8. large intestine
9. anus
10. kidney
11. nephrons
12. ureter
13. urinary bladder
14. urethra

Copyright © by Holt, Rinehart and Winston. All rights reserved.

Name _____ Date _____ Class _____

Alien Anagrams

After you finish reading Chapter 24, give this puzzle a try! A spaceship full of alien ambassadors has just landed in your backyard. They are very interested in earthling science, especially the study of biological systems. Help them translate their scrambled list of terms. DOOG CLUK!

1. long, straight tube connecting your throat and stomach — GAPHOUSES — esophagus
2. microscopic filters located in the kidneys — HORNPENS — nephrons
3. large, reddish brown organ that helps with digestion — VLIRE — liver
4. green liquid used in fat digestion — LEIB — bile
5. rhythmic muscle contractions in the esophagus — STRASPELISI — peristalsis
6. digestion that involves breaking, crushing, and mashing of food — HELNAMACCI — mechanical
7. tube that allows urine to leave the body — HURTEAR — urethra
8. last section of the large intestine — METRUC — rectum
9. muscular organ that squeezes food into chyme — THOSCAM — stomach
10. digestion that involves breaking down large molecules of food into nutrients — CLAMHICE — chemical
11. small, fingerlike projections of the wall of the small intestine — LIVLI — villi
12. organ of the digestive and endocrine systems — SNARPACE — pancreas
13. bean-shaped organs that filter blood — SKYNIED — kidneys
14. baglike organ that stores bile — BALDGLARDLE — gallbladder
15. process of removing waste from the body — RICENOXET — excretion
16. where most chemical digestion occurs — SLALM SEENITINT — small intestine

The Eyes Have It

Complete this worksheet after you finish reading Chapter 25, Section 2.
Match the descriptions in Column B with the correct structure in
Column A, and write the corresponding letter in the appropriate
space. When you have finished, use the words in Column A to label
the diagram.

Column A	Column B
_b_ **1.** rods	**a.** holds the photoreceptors
_d_ **2.** lens	**b.** give a view of the world in grays
_g_ **3.** optic nerve	**c.** changes pupil size to control the amount of light entering
_f_ **4.** cones	**d.** focuses light onto the retina
_c_ **5.** iris	**e.** allows light into the eye
_e_ **6.** pupil	**f.** interpret bright light; give a colorful view of the world
_a_ **7.** retina	**g.** takes impulses from the retina to the brain

The photoreceptors on the
retina _____

are called _____

rods _____ and _____ cones

optic nerve

lens

iris

pupil

Copyright © by Holt, Rinehart and Winston. All rights reserved.

This System Is Just "Two" Nervous! continued

Left Hand: Ouch! Pain! Pain! Spinal Cord, help!

Spinal Cord: Left Hand, stop touching that hot mug!

Cerebellum: Watch out, Legs! Leg Muscles, this is the **Cerebellum**, be
quick about it and step to the side, not to the back! You are about to
trip over the dog!

Cerebrum: Hey, what just happened? I missed it.

Spinal Cord: Don't worry, Cerebrum, it was just another involuntary
movement. The mug we grabbed was too hot to handle, so a reflex
prevented the hands from getting burned. I took care of it since you
are just too slow, but hey, that's my job.

Questions

1. The nervous system is made up of the _____ central _____
   nervous system and the _____ peripheral _____ nervous
   system.

2. The central nervous system is made up of the brain and the
   _____ spinal cord _____.

3. The peripheral nervous system has many _____ nerves _____
   throughout the body.

4. Combing your hair, getting out of bed, and getting dressed are all
   examples of _____ voluntary movement _____.

5. The process of digestion and the pumping your heart does are
   both examples of _____ involuntary movement _____.

6. The neurons in your body use _____ dendrites _____ and
   _____ axons _____ to transfer information.

7. The _____ cerebrum _____ is responsible for thinking and
   memory.

8. The _____ medulla _____ controls your heart rate, blood
   pressure, and involuntary breathing.

9. The _____ cerebellum _____ keeps track of the body's
   position.

10. _____ Motor neurons _____ tell your muscles to move.

11. _____ Sensory neurons _____ use _____ receptors _____ to tell you
    when you are hungry and cold.

Copyright © by Holt, Rinehart and Winston. All rights reserved.

Copyright © by Holt, Rinehart and Winston. All rights reserved.

Copyright © by Holt, Rinehart and Winston. All rights reserved.

Name _____ Date _____ Class _____

Every Gland Lends a Hand

Complete this worksheet after you finish reading Chapter 25, Section 3.

1. How many endocrine glands are discussed in this chapter?

   __8__

2. The __parathyroid__ glands regulate the level of calcium in your blood.

3. Which gland controls blood-sugar levels?

   __pancreas__

4. When your body responds to stress or danger, it uses the __adrenal__ glands.

5. Which one of the glands helps your body fight disease?

   __thymus__

6. Your body uses chemical messengers released into the blood, called __hormones__, to control body functions.

7. The __thyroid__ gland increases the rate at which you use energy.

8. Which glands are involved in reproduction?

   __testes__ or __ovaries__

9. This gland has many functions, one of which is to help the thyroid function properly. Which gland is this?

   __pituitary__

10. All these glands are part of the __endocrine__ system.

11. What are the functions of the endocrine system?

   It is involved in the control of slower, more long term processes such as

   fluid balance, growth, and sexual development.

Copyright © by Holt, Rinehart and Winston. All rights reserved.

Name _____ Date _____ Class _____

Your Body's Own Language

Give this anagram a try after you finish reading Chapter 25!

1. system in your body responsible for gathering and interpreting information about the body's internal and external environment: URSVNEO

   N E R V O U S

2. small snail-shaped organ of the inner ear: CHACOLE

   C O C H L E A

3. subdivision of question 1; includes your brain and spinal cord: ANRCELT

   C E N T R A L

4. subdivision of your nervous system; collection of nerves: LIPPERHARE

   P E R I P H E R A L

5. piece of curved material in the eye that focuses light on the retina: SLEN

   L E N S

6. specialized cells that transfer messages as electrical energy: NENORUS

   N E U R O N S

7. special neurons in your eye that help you see color: SNOCE

   C O N E S

8. short branched extensions through which question 6 receives signals: SERENDDIT

   D E N D R I T E S

9. long cell fiber that transmits information to other cells: NOXA

   A X O N

10. type of neuron that gathers information about what is happening in and around your body: NYSSREO

   S E N S O R Y

11. group of cells that makes special chemicals for your body: GNALD

   G L A N D

12. colored part of the eye: ISRI

   I R I S

13. specialized dendrites that detect changes inside or outside the body: OPETCRSER

   R E C E P T O R S

ANSWER KEY

CHAPTER 26 REINFORCEMENT WORKSHEET

Reproduction Review

Complete this worksheet after you finish reading Chapter 26, Section 1.
Different organisms reproduce in different ways. Fill in the table below by circling the correct type of reproduction. Then indicate the organism's method of fertilization and where the embryo develops. Several boxes have been filled in to get you started.

Organism	Type of reproduction	Method of fertilization	Where the embryo develops
Hydra	asexual or sexual	none	none (no embryo)
Whale	asexual or sexual	internal	inside the mother (placental)
Chicken	asexual or sexual	internal	in eggs outside the mother
Frog	asexual or sexual	internal or external	in eggs outside the mother
Sea star	asexual or sexual	none	none
Echidna	asexual or sexual	internal	in eggs outside the mother
Fish	asexual or sexual	internal or external	in eggs outside the mother
Human	asexual or sexual	internal	inside the mother (placental)
Kangaroo	asexual or sexual	internal	in a pouch outside the mother

Copyright © by Holt, Rinehart and Winston. All rights reserved.

Your Body's Own Language, continued

14. send messages from the brain and spinal cord to other systems:
OMOTR EOSURNN
M O T O R   N E U R O N S

15. axons that are bundled together with blood vessels and connective tissue: NSREVE
N E R V E S

16. the largest organ of the central nervous system: ARNIB
B R A I N

17. chemical messengers produced by the endocrine glands: SHORNMOE
H O R M O N E S

18. part of question 16 where thinking takes place: CREUMBER
C E R E B R U M

19. part of question 16 that helps you keep your balance: MULERBECLE
C E R E B E L L U M

20. transfers electrical impulses from the eye to the brain: COPTI VERNE
O P T I C   N E R V E

21. part of question 16 that connects to the spinal cord: DELUALM
M E D U L L A

22. a quick, involuntary action: FELEXR
R E F L E X

23. system that controls body functions such as sexual development: CODENINER
E N D O C R I N E

24. the light-sensitive layer of cells at the back of the eye: ETNRAI
R E T I N A

25. special neurons in the eye that detect light: EPSERROOPTHTCO
P H O T O R E C E P T O R S

26. electrical messages that pass along the neurons: SPULIMES
I M P U L S E S

27. type of question 25 that can detect very dim light: DSRO
R O D S

Copyright © by Holt, Rinehart and Winston. All rights reserved.

Copyright © by Holt, Rinehart and Winston. All rights reserved.

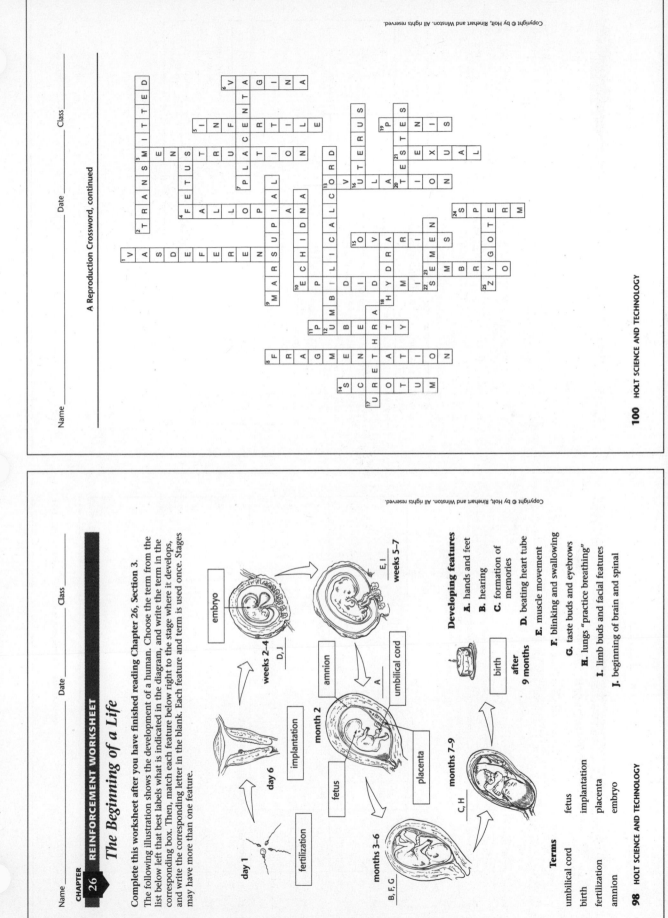

Copyright © by Holt, Rinehart and Winston. All rights reserved.

Copyright © by Holt, Rinehart and Winston. All rights reserved.

Name _____ Date _____ Class _____

VOCABULARY REVIEW WORKSHEET

Puzzle-itis Vaccine

After finishing Chapter 27, give this puzzle a try!

In the space provided at right, write the vocabulary term that best matches the clue given. Then write the circled letters in the boxes at the bottom of the page to reveal a purpose of the immune system.

1. type of disease in which the body attacks its own cells — A U T O I M M U N E

2. kill cells infected with a pathogen — K I L L E R T C E L L S

3. resistance to a disease — I M M U N I T Y

4. "remember" how to make antibodies for a specific pathogen — M E M O R Y B C E L L S

5. substance that kills or slows down the growth of bacteria — A N T I B I O T I C

6. disease in which cells divide at an uncontrolled rate — C A N C E R

7. the overreaction of the immune system to harmless antigens — A L L E R G Y

8. the body system that attacks pathogens — I M M U N E S Y S T E M

9. cells that produce antibodies — B C E L L S

10. special protein that attaches to a specific pathogen — A N T I B O D Y

11. small piece of a pathogen that generates an immune response — A N T I G E N

12. diseases that spread from one living thing to another — I N F E C T I O U S

13. agent that causes an infectious disease — P A T H O G E N

14. cells that engulf microorganisms or viruses — M A C R O P H A G E

15. use of heat to kill bacteria in food and beverages — P A S T E U R I Z A T I O N

16. send word to killer T cells and activate B cells — H E L P E R T C E L L

A purpose of the immune system is to:

E L I M I N A T E   D I S E A S E

Copyright © by Holt, Rinehart and Winston. All rights reserved.

Name _____ Date _____ Class _____

REINFORCEMENT WORKSHEET

Immunity Teamwork

Complete this worksheet after reading Chapter 27, Section 2.

Your immune system works because many different types of cells work together to kill pathogens. Listed in the table below are the different cells of the immune system. Next to each of them, write a role they play in curing an infection.

Cells	How they help get rid of disease
Macrophages	Sample answers: Macrophages engulf pathogens that invade the body. They display antigens on their cell membranes so that other cells will recognize an infection is taking place. They also eat up any pathogens tagged with antibodies.
Helper T cells	Sample answers: Helper T cells are activated by the antigens displayed by the macrophages. They tell the killer T cells to kill cells with these antigens. They also activate B cells to make antibodies.
Killer T cells	Killer T cells kill any cell infected with the pathogens.
B cells	B cells produce millions of antibodies.
Antibodies	Sample answers: Antibodies cling to antigens. They mark antigens so immune cells and proteins swarm to attack them.

Copyright © by Holt, Rinehart and Winston. All rights reserved.

Copyright © by Holt, Rinehart and Winston. All rights reserved.

Name _____ Date _____ Class _____

To Eat or Not to Eat . . .

Complete this worksheet after reading Chapter 28, Section 1.
Put together a balanced diet for a day. Choose one breakfast, one lunch, and one dinner from the menus below. (Assume that the portion sizes will be adjusted so you receive the correct amount of calories. Focus on selecting a balanced diet.)

Menus

	1	2	3
Breakfast	scrambled eggs bacon orange juice milk	blueberry muffin toast (with strawberry jam) orange juice milk	skip breakfast
Lunch	black bean soup pear spinach salad milk	ham-and-cheese sandwich (on rye bread) carrot sticks banana milk	cheeseburger French fries pickle soda
Dinner	spaghetti (with tomato sauce) garlic bread tofu green beans milk	sausage-and-pepperoni pizza soda	baked chicken breast rice pilaf salad dinner roll broccoli milk

1. Record the meals you chose for your healthy diet in the spaces below.

Breakfast # _____ Lunch # _____ Dinner # _____ Best answers: 2,2,3;2,1,3;2,1,1

2. Why did you make those choices?

Answers will vary but should focus on getting a balance of food from different levels of the food pyramid. Sample answer: I chose these meals because I would eat a variety of breads, fruits, and vegetables, but not so much meat.

Copyright © by Holt, Rinehart and Winston. All rights reserved.

Name _____ Date _____ Class _____

To Eat, or Not to Eat . . . , continued

3. Just for fun, choose the worst diet. Again, pick one breakfast, lunch, and dinner.

Breakfast # _____ Lunch # _____ Dinner # _____ Best answers: 3,3,2;1,3,2

4. What problems would people who eat like this face?

Answers will vary. Sample answer: They would become obese from eating excess fat and Calories and suffer from malnutrition due to lack of nutrients.

5. Some people prefer not to eat meat. Can you find a healthy vegetarian alternative among the choices? (Hint: Look at the category that includes meat in the food pyramid—it also contains nonmeat items.)

Breakfast # _____ Lunch # _____ Dinner # _____ Answer: 2,1,1

6. What are your favorite foods for breakfast, lunch, and dinner? (There are no right or wrong answers; write down what you really like.) Write your choices in the boxes below.

Breakfast	Lunch	Dinner

7. What could you do to make your favorite meals healthier? (Hint: You can add, subtract, or substitute foods in your diet.)

Answers will vary, but should focus on including neglected food groups and limiting food groups that are overrepresented in their favorites (especially sweets and fat). Sample answer: I would try to eat more vegetables and order my turkey subs on a whole-wheat bun.

8. What are water's main functions in the body? (Circle all that apply.)

(a.) It transports substances.
(b.) It helps regulate temperature.
(c.) It provides lubrication.
d. It breaks down fats.

Copyright © by Holt, Rinehart and Winston. All rights reserved.

Copyright © by Holt, Rinehart and Winston. All rights reserved.

Name _____ Date _____ Class _____

CHAPTER 28 VOCABULARY REVIEW WORKSHEET

Hidden Health Message

After reading Chapter 28, complete this worksheet.
Circle the best answer for each question. Add that answer, next to the appropriate number, to the hidden message puzzle on the next page. The first question has been done for you as an example.

1. any substance that must be consumed to promote normal growth, maintenance, and repair
   (nutrients) minerals vitamins

2. organic compounds that are essential, in small quantities, for good health
   nutrients minerals (vitamins)

3. inorganic elements that are essential, in small quantities, for good health
   nutrients (minerals) vitamins

4. organic compounds, composed of amino acids, that are used to build and repair body parts
   (proteins) carbohydrates cholesterols

5. organic compounds, made of sugars, that give the body energy
   proteins (carbohydrates) cholesterols

6. a type of fat known to raise blood cholesterol levels
   vitamin unsaturated (saturated)

7. a type of fat that may help reduce blood cholesterol levels
   vitamin (unsaturated) saturated

8. a disorder caused by consuming more Calories than are burned
   anorexia malnutrition (obesity)

9. a disorder resulting from consuming the wrong combination of nutrients
   (malnutrition) bulimia anorexia

10. a disorder caused by self-starvation
    malnutrition bulimia (anorexia)

11. a disorder caused by binge eating followed by induced vomiting
    malnutrition (bulimia) anorexia

12. any chemical substance that causes a physical or emotional change in a person
    (drug) mineral vitamin

REINFORCEMENT & VOCABULARY REVIEW WORKSHEETS **105**

Copyright © by Holt, Rinehart and Winston. All rights reserved.

Name _____ Date _____ Class _____

Hidden Health Message, continued

13. a drug prepared from opium
    nutrient (narcotic) nicotine

14. a chemical stimulant from tobacco leaves
    nutrient narcotic (nicotine)

15. a disease in which a person is addicted to alcohol
    alcoholic (alcoholism) REM sleep

16. physical and mental response to situations that create pressure
    tolerance (stress) sleep

Hidden-message puzzle
Complete this puzzle to find out one thing you need to be healthy.

Puzzle answers filled in:
5 CARBOHYDRATES
15 ALCOHOLISM
1 NUTRIENTS
4 PROTEINS
6 SATURATED
8 OBESITY
12 DRUG
10 ANOREXIA
11 BULIMIA
13 NARCOTIC
9 MALNUTRITION
2 VITAMINS
14 NICOTINE
3 MINERALS
16 STRESS
7 UNSATURATED

106 HOLT SCIENCE AND TECHNOLOGY
